the incompleteness book

Edited by

Julia Prendergast
Shane Strange
Jen Webb

RECENT WORK PRESS

AAWP
Australasian Association of Writing Programs

First published in 2020 by
TEXT: Journal of Writing and Writing Courses & Recent Work Press

Publication editors: Julia Prendergast, Shane Strange, Jen Webb

Publication design and layout: Caren Florance

ISBN: 978-0-6488343-8-0

Cover image: Malcolm, 'Theatrical mask street art on a wall in South Calgary', 2017. Flickr: https://www.flickr.com/photos/18946008@N06/38645894341.

CONTENTS

INTRODUCTION

Julia Prendergast

The Incompleteness Book is the result of a call for contributions to the theme: the incompleteness of human experience. The call was distributed in April 2020, amidst the global pandemic of COVID-19. The theme seemed apt, although (disclaimer) I'm biased on this one – I think anything worthwhile I've ever written is about the incompleteness of human experience. Or perhaps I feel that human experience is necessarily incomplete. Maybe there is little difference and I will try not to prevaricate, too much, although I often do. 'Get there faster,' my eldest daughter says.

In any event, if I felt that human experience was incomplete *before*. . .

I decided to write this introduction during the submission window. I hoped it would speak about what writing can do to us and for us or, at the very least, what the contributions to this book did to me and for me. What was to be a short introduction became a personal essay, which is not really my style (like, not at all). Only, who chooses?

I don't want to 'front-face' a book of fine (short) contributions with a (long) personal essay. The contributions speak for themselves. Having said that, I'm aware that I would not have written the essay if it weren't for the contributions to the book. If it belongs anywhere, perhaps it is here. And so, I attach it as an afterword for you to take or leave as you wish. I'm deeply interested in what this climate does to our writing. The essay is an attempt to articulate that, in response to the contributions to this book, and the conversations around it, although I'm not sure what I came up with is altogether articulate – and I'm wondering if perhaps that's okay – if, like the contributions themselves, this is a gesture of 'thinking positions' and incompleteness, across a narrow window of time.

Each night, across the submission window, I read the new contributions. The entries themselves, together with the messages from authors, have broken me and sustained me during these early weeks of home exile. Perhaps that sounds melodramatic, or at least tipping the scales for emotional intensity, but it is nevertheless true, and I am, nevertheless, emotionally intense. Many of the submissions swallowed me whole and informed my dreams and my writing. Are there many things as precious? Writing generating writing – the binding sinews of connectivity that *is* word art. . .

Being cooped up in this hot, tiny apartment for weeks has often given me a headache, but not today. I am reading *Letters to Sartre* by de Beauvoir, which I find terrific but too emotional beneath its air of frantic obsessions. And with self-isolating just beginning, there remains a vague fear of expecting too much from that recovery of life.

Now my spirits are as sombre as the night itself. As I try to distract myself by chopping and frying the remaining butterflied lamb leg from the refrigerator, a fear of craving, disappointment, and tension immediately emerge. I keep wondering if there is comfort in being glum and hopeless.

I dial a number, and Jayanti's smiling face appears on the screen. While we chat, she gives me a tour around her house via Skype. 'Hubby's doing grocery shopping.'

Jayanti's living room has a large sofa, but her children are sitting on the floor with their backs to it. Gadgets and toys scattered around them. She wears her hair in a loose bun and is holding a large plate of rice with thick-sauce dishes. She smiles at me and says, 'This is how it is in our family. We're a tight-knit bunch! We love spending time with each other.'

'Aw,' I say. 'That's really lovely. What did you cook?'

'Fried duck and sweet spicy black squid.'

With her left hand holding the plate, her bony fingers start scooping a small handful of rice mixed with bits of dishes and then tucking it into her eldest daughter's mouth, who has been scrolling down on her phone. She patiently repeats this to her son, who has been sitting cross-legged on the floor with his face hidden behind his laptop. Jayanti again repeats this to her two younger ones, whose eyes are glued to a cartoon show.

When she sees that her son's hand shoots up to snatch a potato chip, she immediately strikes it. 'Never eat anything with your left hand, son – it is dirty. Have I told you many times? You eat with your right hand, you wipe yourself in the toilet with the left.'

'You sound exactly like my mom, Yan. Haven't called her for two weeks.'

'*Lho, piye to*? Call her now! Ask how she's doing. Shower her with love.'

'Yeah, yeah, will do.' I thank her, hang up, and dial another number.

He sleeps in rough four/four time: wake, sleep, dream, wake. He has a nightmare about 'it's' versus 'its'. He has a dream about the ocean: the waves slap him, a rip tugs at his heartstrings, the grey bulge he takes to be seaweed is a killer dolphin that toys with him for days before taking his photo, posting it on Instagram, and eating him. He dreams he is a celebrity: everybody wants to touch him. He dreams about all the people at his local supermarket, bumping about, blockading the aisles, leaning on him and licking him and stealing the last packet of dried yeast from his trolley. He dreams he has moved to Mars: the view is nice if you like oblivion but it's a party planet and he hates techno and he's never lonelier than when he's in a crowd. He dreams there is a shortage of Jatz biscuits.

He works from home, just him and a Dell and the monitor he swiped from the office and the thirty-seven apps he has downloaded so he can talk to his workmates. He plants onion seeds but doesn't think to water them. He dusts off his steel-stringed guitar: he can still play the first half of that Neil Young song about the twentieth century but he's completely forgotten that Michelle Shocked number about Antarctica. He counts his coffee beans twice a day. He washes his hands with laundry powder because he worries he'll run out of soap. He stands on the back lawn and gazes upon the rainwater tank and wonders if he should breed trout. He pours draino down the sink once a week because he's heard that plumbers aren't allowed. He takes his guitar into the shower with him because that's where he does his best singing. He washes the windows then wishes he hadn't. He ignores Easter, but that's nothing new. He gives Frank Sinatra another go but he still doesn't see what all the fuss is about. He levitates: it's good for his core.

for Simon H

Any granola experts out there? Recognizing teenaged
depression? Making puffed rice? Are bidets
really worth owning? Is the existence of fright
kind of following the coast? Is that an urn taxiing along

depression? Making puffed rice? Are bidets
crusting the precipice, this curve that cannot be
kind of following the coast? Is that an urn taxiing along
saying it any different? Two public servants boat,

crusting the precipice, this curve that cannot be
sunk in visionary epidemiology, editing stored files.
Saying it any different? Two public servants boat
but their employers are not objective! Not

sunk in visionary epidemiology, editing stored data
that stays where it crashes. Look to the unfolded back,
but their employers are not objective! Not
once commented on it! People destroy everything

that stays where it crashes. Look to the unfolded back
of my dorsal tongue. People find some issues in it –
once commented on it. People destroy everything,
all sequences: useless on the medium low heat

of my dorsal tongue. People find some issues in it.
Holy restarts every day, knocking around
all sequences: useless on the medium low heat,
ghosts of a ventilated saviour complex.

Holy restarts every day, knocking around
granola experts out there, recognizing teenaged
ghosts of a ventilated saviour complex
really worth owning. Is the existence of fright?

EXT. AERIAL - SYDNEY HARBOUR BRIDGE - DUSK

JADE (V.O.)

They won't send up a juicer.

EXT. HOTEL - DUSK

Cops stand guard.

KELLY (V.O.)
You're gonna stab him, with a butter knife, then cut him up, with a butter knife?

INT. HOTEL CORRIDOR - EVENING

Fabulous hotel. Three rooms have doors open. A woman sits at each doorway.

JADE
Fine for you, your Aden got taken to ICU.

RACHEL
Jade.

KELLY
Nah. It's true. He shits me like you wouldn't believe. You think Carole got the idea from Fargo?

JADE
The wood-chipper?

Kelly nods. They consider.

RACHEL

Ahh.

(gets up)

Cramp. They'll notice he's missing.

Rachel stretches, an alarm sounds. Rachel steps back.

JADE

Shit.

Silence.

They all start breathing again. Another door opens.

KELLY

Here we go.

SARA

You heard the cops. They have to come up again, they'll arrest everyone on this floor.

JADE

(reads off phone)

There's a new episode, next week.

KELLY

None of the main ones are in it.

SARA

Hell really is other people.

KELLY
Hello. We don't like you either.

RACHEL
(breaks tension)
So... Dr Fauci says things won't be normal again till November.

KELLY
Eight months till I wear jeans again.

JADE
So much Netflix.

SARA
It's a chance to re-set society. We should spend this time thinking-

They all groan.

SARA
-Thinking about what kind of society we want to restart in 6 or 8 months. No racism, no sexism-

KELLY
(sarcastic)
Oh. Yeah. A pandemic was totally the ingredient missing.
(waves imaginary wand)
Equality. World Peace.

SARA
So, you're just not even gonna

bother considering it. At all? What about the clean air? The reduction in pollution over eight months. Imagine.

KELLY

Ugh. That song- Don't get me started on celebrity lockdown hot messes.

EXT. VENICE - WATERWAYS - DAY

SARA (V.O.)

In Venice the water's so clear, you can see-

KELLY (V.O.)

I thought they were way deeper.

EXT. DOWNTOWN LAS VEGAS - DAY

SARA (V.O.)

No smog in L.A.

KELLY (V.O.)

Seriously, why'd you leave?

INT. CORRIDOR - EVENING

KELLY

Not like anyone wants you here.

Jade and Rachel look at Kelly.

KELLY

Don't even. You were thinking it.

Beat.

RACHEL

Would be cool, though. Getting paid the same as every mediocre white guy.

JADE

Considered for every promotion.

KELLY

I'm still wearing makeup.

Bing.

JADE

Fork.

They disappear, doors close.

Silence.

The lift doors open.

THE END

I'm obsessed with Spanish things: cava, Velazquez's *Las Meninas* and *pulpo con espuma de patata* at En Busca de Tiempo. I dance Flamenco while I sprinkle smoked paprika on my eggs and whisper 'Run Moon run Moon Moon', as you untie my espadrilles. When you tell me the Spanish Flu wasn't Spanish, I lie on your side of the bed and write prose poems to prevent lack of oxygen to my heart.

the silence is as quartz is, pale & light-fractured,
gleaming like mounds of sugar or the substance of death.
beyond the frightfully even valley of it is a jagged sky,
the clouds a dark-lit gravel, & in the water sheeting
down from them is the memory of your skin:
fish-glimmer & salted wounds, complete & ineffectual
as time or a child's grip.

Most autumns, we continue to harvest produce from our summer garden. At an altitude of over 1,100 metres, gardening on the Northern Tablelands of New South Wales means adjusting expectations to what can thrive in the sunny, but mild, summers. It also means being eternally optimistic, as even December nights can be very chilly and hard frosts can begin in March. This April, the days are clear and the nights aren't cold. Yet, the usual lush beds of tomatoes, radishes, basil, aubergines, rhubarb, melons and parsley are nowhere to be seen.

In 2018, the region received less than two-thirds of the long-term average rainfall. In 2019, less than one-third, making it both the driest, and the warmest, year on record. We hosed, then lugged watering cans, but our tanks sank so low that soon all we had to offer were the buckets of suds saved from short, short showers and the meagre washing up.

Then, all of New England was aflame, and any remaining energy went into preparing for a fire. One hot blustery morning, a wall of flame duly swept down from the adjacent national park and across the entire farm. By their skill and by their sweat, the firefighters saved our sheep, our horses and the house. Afterwards, the skies remained cloudless. We joked we were safe from the fire threat as there was nothing left to burn, but we weren't laughing.

And then it rained and kept raining. The deluge put out the surrounding fires, many of which had smouldered on for months. The storms filled the dams and the tanks. The gums sprouted new leaves and the native grasses spread across the paddocks, vivid against the drifts of black ash.

One day, we saw that a mass of rich green purslane (*Portulaca oleracea*), that lemony native succulent, was growing between the garden beds. Appreciated by Indigenous Australians and early immigrants but largely classed as a weed in Australia today, we chopped armfuls into salads and sautéed the stems with garlic. Foraging for the crispest new shoots, we noticed that other plants were treating the late summer like early spring and coming to life in the grass-filled beds. Weeding revealed masses of leggy coriander, a dozen cherry tomato plants, new stems of disco-pink rhubarb, a bed of nuggety black radishes, tiny heads of parsley, too-much fragrant tarragon.

Their success all depends on when it frosts but, this year, we are also planting a winter garden into those now-weeded beds, sowing broccoli, spring onions, celeriac and leeks. One bed, however, is dedicated to the now gone-to-seed purslane.

Purslane Salad

Gather, gently rinse, and chop purslane stems and leaves into bite-sized lengths.

Dress with a garlicky vinaigrette made with wine or cider vinegar and good olive oil, seasoned with ground black pepper to taste.

Diced tomatoes make a tasty addition to the salad, as does a dab of Dijon mustard in the dressing.

See, all it takes is me saying, don't hunch your shoulders while you're watching tv, you'll get a sore back. She sits there up close, her shoulders scrunched and her eyes tightly focused. I can see her bones jutting out of her bright blue dressing-gown. I worry about how much she can see; how she keeps moving closer to that television. I interrupt her in the middle of *Gladiator* which she says at one point was a bit gruesome. She swivels her head round as I'm heading out the door after saying what I said about her shoulders and says sharply – 'when are you going home' in a tone which says – half-jokingly – I think you should go now. She doesn't like being told things about her shoulders; doesn't like it when I say don't forget to wash your hands when you get back home from your walk. I think of my father who always used to say to my mother – you can be told Dorrie but not much. I think he used to say that to me too. I leave, hoping she relaxes those shoulders in spite of herself; hoping someday soon I'll be able to shake her.

In 1995, my father, wearing nothing but red underpants, killed a man on La Perouse Beach. Twenty-three years later, the first thing I see on La Perouse beach is a pot-bellied man in a hot red thong putting rubbish in a bin. I gawk, wondering if this could be him.

The bay is dotted like fairy bread with rainbow umbrellas and bright bikinis. I throw out my towel and watch buried stories tease from shifting sands with tiny feet. The water winks, the day is clear. I shimmy into my swimmers underneath my dress.

One bulbous rock protrudes from the sand – a giant clam shell in Sandro Botticelli's painting, Birth of Venus. The goddess, Venus, stands on the clam naked, hands at her bits, hair snaking to her crotch. Her body is fully matured yet she was born underwater moments before. She has emerged from the sea.

I can see myself on that rock. Arms to the sun, hairy – free. I drop my dress and run to the water.

Underwater, I see Mum drinking alone. I left to work at an outdoor theatre company. The director was my friend.

'You need to get away,' the director said.

Underwater, I see Mum swaying in her chair looking at the ghosts of things hanging in the frangipani: a rusted chandelier, a giant heart with a dint, caged fairy lights that don't brighten, and Jase, her late partner.

'Come home,' Mum pleaded.

Underwater, I was warm.

Later, in the middle of a pandemic, I'll see the rope scar on the frangipani.

'You haven't seen it?' Juzzie, my could-have-been aunty, turns to me wide-eyed.

We sit in yellow chairs 1.5 metres apart with a bottle between us. She starts pointing before she gets up. I follow her crooked arm. It pulls us in, I feel her breath. It's close. I see Jase gliding along the surface like a ballerina in pointe shoes. Matters of an inch. We've broken the law, our shoulders are touching. We back into our chairs. Soon, she backs out of my driveway.

Under the scar, I close my eyes. I never let Jase play father, my father left me at La Perouse and I'm sipping its waters. I roll the salt about my tongue and line my stomach. First, I thought it was for answers then reclamation. Perhaps it's closeness – letting myself be within an inch.

A hundred years separates me from the protagonist of my in-progress bio-fiction novel. A hundred years separates all of us from the last viral pandemic. I pause and reflect on how it would have been for the essayist, novelist and social theorist, Olive Schreiner, who lived in London during the influenza pandemic of 1918-19. She did not contract the disease that killed more people than the Great War, a quarter of a million dying in Britain alone. Unlike COVID-19, the influenza epidemic was merciless in selecting young adults rather than the old as its victims. Olive was 63. I wondered what her life would have been like during the crisis, what deprivations she might have suffered, what travel plans may have been curtailed and, importantly, how did the pandemic impact her ability to write?

I dipped into Olive's epistolary and was surprised in reading through her letters across these years to find scant reference to the pandemic. A grand-nephew, a soldier recently returned from the Front and camped at the military base at Aldershot in Hampshire, had contracted influenza and died. Her letter to her good friend, Alice Greene, notes that 'Influenza seems raging in the camps here.' She didn't attend the funeral because she found out too late to travel there. Reporting of the pandemic was restricted by wartime censorship where the morale of the population was apparently considered more important than its health. Thus, little was publicly known of the extent or voracity of the virus brought home to civilians by returning soldiers. Suffering asthma and angina, Olive did not venture out to join Londoners who gathered in their thousands at the victory celebrations that ran from November 1918 to July 1919. A confirmed pacifist who had supported conscientious objectors and lost faith in her old friend Edward Carpenter and her South African associate Mohandas Gandhi – both supporters of the War – it is unlikely she would have wanted to attend. The contagion ripped through the thronging crowds like wildfire.

Olive suffered deprivations: rampant inflation and food rationing, 'half an ounce of butter per week' and no meat, but 'what others (in Germany) have gone through in the way of starvation [...]

makes my dry bread and milkless tea stick in my throat.' She found new books to read – *The Diary of a Dead Soldier*, and John Maynard Keynes' *The Economic Consequences of the Peace* – she thought as good as the writings of John Stuart Mill. During her self-imposed isolation, Olive stayed in touch with family and friends through letter writing, and she composed her last literary gift to the world, *The Dawn of Civilization*.

This year, 2020, marks the one-hundredth anniversary of Olive Schreiner's passing. A writers' festival in her honour was to be held in South Africa and, with enthusiasm, I accepted an invitation to attend as a speaker. Then, COVID-19 came along and the government slapped on a travel ban. My protagonist smiles at me with irony, and I return her smile.

JOURNAL, EASTER MONDAY 2020

Rebekah Clarkson

Go for a walk. You should go for a walk. Truly, a walk. Walking is good. Take a walk. Could you go for a walk? Go for a short walk. I'm going for a walk; you should go for a walk. Why don't you go for a walk? May I suggest a walk? Go for a walk, in nature, if you can. Get out and go for a walk. Oh, I'm sorry. That's right, I forgot, you broke your foot. Yeah, right. Smell this. You should smell this. Have you smelt this? This is exquisite; you should smell it. Try this. Smell that. Go for a walk. Oh, this smells so good; try it. Smell this. Do you love this? I love this. Oh fuck, sorry. Oh my god, I always forget; you can't smell. Sorry. Shit. I'm the worst. The problem with depression: ultimately, it's annoying for everybody, because it's not interesting but nor is it straightforward. It's annoyingly not interesting and not straightforward. There is no answer and there is no solution. It just goes on and on and up and down and on and on and around and around. I don't know where to get the answer. There is no answer. Sorry. Today I have no more ideas. But look: the day is cool and sunny, perfectly Autumnal. Birds tweet and chirp. The tangle of metal tags tinkle on the dog's collar. Leaves sway gently on branch fingers; limbs hold still. Faint echo of small dogs barking in the distance. Low hum of a car engine revving up a register, changing gears. Friends drop off. Family grow tired. Flowers bloom.

Here's what I'm thinking, for better or worse: if it weren't for the thing – and I don't blame you for it – then I think we could do okay at this. That's all. But what would I know? What would I know.

FLATTEN

Katharine Coles

If this arc could be as long
As justice's, as flat. Until then

Failure lies in it, and hope: the tree
Laden with snow, boughs

Flexing as weight accumulates until
They have no grace left; the road

That follows only where land
Permits in its geologic rigor: down

The canyon, following every hard
Twist the creek takes in carving

Itself through time. In turn, we follow
The water as it goes, under trees

No longer weighted but still winter
-minded and bare, spring surging

But invisible in them. I straighten
My back under what it bears:

Food and water, heavier
Than it looks, my mood, all

I know. Under its own weight still
My back bends. Without touching,

We bow, each one to the other
In gesture place our hope.

WE'RE ALL AFRAID OF THE DARK

Katharine Coles

We didn't used to be, at least
I thought I wasn't. And now

I fear small things too, not like
The dark, so large it's everywhere,

But a gnat, more than anything
Just pesky; a mote or mite of dust;

A word. Today, I wash my hands
The way the government tells me

And leave the house only to run
Long corridors of wind

Alone. The wind can't hurt me,
I think, being invisible, being I move

Right through it. Until it fills
Itself, until it turns

And howls and doesn't so much
Lift the roof from the house

Next-door as become that roof
In flight. It must, of course,

Come down, the roof. That's
A problem. Not the only one.

Is it a poetics of feminist rage? Is it about what it is to have a body? A rage body. Feminist about body. Your body? Is it answering a question about body that can't be explored in words? Explore rage. Feminist exploration body. Subject does object. Feminist does what? Explode anger. Is anger abject? An aberration in body. In a woman's body. Un-allowed. Is it? Is it trying? What is it trying? Try body. Try rage. Try feminist. What is a feminist trying to do? Do feminism. Have an un-allowed body. What to do with it? Anything? Make with it? Make of it? Can it make? Can feminism make? Can poetics make? Can rage make? Make rage body. Would a rage body shake? What would it feel like? To shake a body. To make feminist body. How would it feel and how would you write it? Remember body. Shake body. Try and make a shape of it. What can it do? Anything? Can the make shake body make anything happen? Can feminist happen to a body? Can body happen to poetics? Can rage make body feminist? Can poetics happen to rage? What can a feminist body make? How is happening made? By what it is not? What is made between a thing and its opposite? What is the opposite of feminist? Make up a feminist. Opposite a body. There is something between the thing and its opposite. In the place between a thing and an un-thing. It is probably anger. Because it has trouble telling what it is. It tries to shout but has no words. It rages. How then to write it? How to make words out of no words? Try. Is this it?

It's a parade of cars and a sidewalk of teachers. They're standing three metres apart. Some wear Book Week costumes, others hold streamers. I've taken turns being in love with all of them – the kindergarten teacher, now the principal; the Star Trek-inspired brainiac my son had for years three and five; the sports-lover in running shoes from year two. They're all there, waving, while cars honk and children lean out of windows. My son begs me to stop crying but my head is dizzy and the seat belt has locked me in. We pause at the crosswalk, so close to yesterday on this suburban street. It's the ritual of dropping him at school that I miss – the morning assembly, the smallest of talk with other mothers and carers.

We sit in front of the fire – two metres apart, then 1.5 – when night drops. The back fence is being replaced and we're burning the ragged, grey palings. The flames ease and those neon-orange coals glimmer. If I look up, I can see into her yard: the outline of a Hills Hoist, the shed leaning to one side. She's younger than me by a couple of years, a nurse in ED at the hospital down south. She's holding a mug with whiskey and I'm working through a bottle of red and even so, even at this late hour, I'm counting the centimetres between us. She's ventilated crewmembers from that ship parked just beyond our harbour. When she gets home from work, she strips off her scrubs, naked in the backyard, before using the outside shower. I thought her proximity, sitting here on a milk crate, might scare me but it's a relief: if anything jumps between us, I'll be a recipient, not a donor. I know it doesn't end there, I know that, but I think of last night and the drunk teenagers running up and down the street in front of my house, screaming at the night. I edge closer to her, aware that I'm one of those kids and I'm also the middle-aged parent who lets his child scooter with friends, and I'm that boomer standing in front of me at the supermarket, refusing to relinquish the privilege of pushing up in line.

WHAT SEPARATES A COBWEB AND A SPIDERWEB

Dave Drayton

---

what separates a cobweb and   a spiderweb is
a spread sheet if   working from home

a petal settles her
a pet'll settle her

termites feast on   a hermit at the wedding
family tree   takes advantage of the catering

a
hatchling
hatching
a plan

vacating yesterday with   a quiver and a bath
frozen compilations   backstage thermometers

the shaving newsmen
& the freshwater newspapers

trees and sandstone   of the lawn's rage
stand regardless   of homogeneous garbage

a wood Samaritan

to remember the good one

whose knuckles met the

door five times that day

whose uncles' ties

all look the same
who decline

who'd decline

a cuppa

honestly

Last night I dreamt about my sister. In the dream, she and two other people were putting together a compensation claim against a hotel a police officer had taken them to. She had thinned right down. Afterwards, when it was just the two of us in the room, she said, she'd taken the thing she'd taken because she could. Crying, I begged her to look after her two-year-old. She then cried herself, not knowing that I cared.

Earlier or later in the dream, older people who were highly educated and who wore heavy grey and red woollen pants and coats said, the problem with being too educated now is that people ask you to lead. One of them then said, the other problem is, people comment on your garments.

My mother has had my sister's two-year-old now for almost two months.

A few weeks ago my father phoned to say he'd had a bad fever for a few days. At night, he said, he would have fever dreams. He was, he said, exhausted. He would try and get a test tomorrow, he said. When I was talking to my mother later that week she said he now had a bad cold. She'd left the two-year-old at daycare once, she said, while she gave a young woman a potting lesson and he'd brought it home. Imagine, she said, dying over a potting lesson. She said, she only has trouble breathing when she's lying down. I said, phone a GP. No, she said. She said, she'd already tried to call the daycare centre, but no one had answered. I said again, phone a GP. After I got off the phone I messaged a friend who had trained to specialise as a GP in the hills around where she lives to ask if he can recommend someone there. He sent a name through, and I sent it to her. I'm okay, she replied back. The following day when I phoned her, she said, I'm all right now, I slept well, finally, and it's cleared away.

For the first few weeks, I spoke to my mother every day or two. She told me how much of a joy the two-year-old is, or is becoming. She said he's just like a boy out of an old picture book. There's no trace of his parents, she said. She said, he looks just the way eldest brother – her first child – had looked at that age. When they wake up, she said, they wrestle playfully, and then he pulls a big long sad face. She then pulls the same big long sad face and he lights up with laughter.

Today a friend called me to ask if my partner and I were okay and to tell me that he and his wife are having a boy. After I answered, I slid on a pair of boots and went out and stood in the carpark behind our apartment where the reception is better. He said that he's been trying to write fictionalised apology letters for men who have been caught out. At first, he said, I just thought it would be funny, something to do with all this time we have. He said he'd been doing some substitute teaching, which, he said, was better than he'd expected. It was well paid, he said, and he was able to do some technical drawings for his renovation while his students worked. But now, he said, his wife has said she doesn't want him out teaching until they have the child. She herself is an obstetrician in a hospital, but, he explained, she is being prevented from having to see anyone who could have come in contact with the virus due to her pregnancy, even though it's understood there is no real threat to pregnancies. As he spoke, I walked around the carpark, following the cracks in the asphalt, as I often did when I spoke to my parents. Then he said, after he'd written a couple of letters, he started thinking more and more about the technical challenge the letters presented him. He said, I tried to really think about, on one hand, the hurt that I had caused in different ways to different people, some of whom I still cared for or couldn't stop myself from caring for, he said, and some of whom I loathed but had once cared for and who had then also cared for me, but also, he said, I tried to feel terrified about my own professional and personal life which I've either just lost or would likely be about to lose, and about my immediate family, who I could also lose. I want the letters, he said, to acknowledge, to a degree, the pain I had caused, or at least not ignore that pain, but, he said, be guided, primarily, by fear. The letters should also, he said, be written with an anger that cannot, he said, quite be detected, or can only be detected, he said, by people who know me personally. He said he couldn't care less if it's a boy or a girl.

NOTE TO SELF (IN NOVEL TIMES)

Willo Drummond

Remember   to love
the world.   Love
the wailing,   rolling world;
the air;   the wildness
of wind   lifting a million kites
of change.

                Love
the deep,   challenging dark
of water;   the topography
                of spirit:
                        a wheatfield
                        a canyon
                        an undulating plateau;

that human   dream
of time   and space
lean into   *that,*
                and this:

the singular   note
of your human heart
calling,   calling
you home

March, 2020

* *'Love yourself. Then forget it. Then, love the world.'*
Mary Oliver, 'To Begin With, the Sweet Grass'.

I've been living in my own kind of isolation since my love stopped breathing, eight months ago. With his death, I became a single mother to a five-month-old. The world instantly closed in around me and my child, our future hanging in a pause.

It seemed so strange that each day I would wake up to grapple again with the numbing horror of his absence and try so hard not to fail at parenting, while the rest of the world acted as though nothing had changed. The sun continued to rise and set. My lungs continued to take in air without any motivation on my part.

So, when news of a virus reached us and then a global pandemic was declared, everything was already upside-down. In a haze of grief, I had devised a hectic weekly schedule of distractions just to get us out of the house, none of which I felt like attending. Advice to stay at home brought some kind of relief. It was easy to shut the door.

But I have found, with no adventures to distract me, I am unable to avoid my grief, and it becomes more insistent every day. It follows me through the rooms of the house, wails at night.

A call from my bereavement counsellor last week helped ground me. It's going to be the hardest time yet, these next four months, she told me. Anticipation of the anniversary; it catches a lot of people off guard, she said. It will be a long, tough winter. You just have to work on getting through each day and focus on the new ahead: the eventual arrival of spring.

Beyond my personal grief, so much of the world is grieving and isolated, mourning the loss of lives, jobs, human contact.

I have never found solace in shared pain.

In the evenings, as I rock my son to sleep, I watch from my lounge room windows as the metro trains pass. They still run on schedule, every half hour, but the lighted carriages sliding through the darkness are all empty.

A friend referred to the pandemic as The Great Pause. It's a fitting name. Grief distorts time and demands of us patience and stillness and sometimes a focus on nothing more and nothing less than each breath in and breath out. And the pause in between. We are all waiting for spring.

ISOLATION TIP #54: TALK TO A GOD YOU DON'T BELIEVE IN

Christie Fogarty

Sunlight bakes her naked toes, and she is content. *This is wrong*, the voice whispers, but she rolls up her pant legs and slides further down the wicker chair, thick fibres scratching up her back. Autumn sunlight hits different. Dry heat, but more than that. Crackling heat; even the waves thrown from fire weren't this crisp.

In this light, all leg hair looks blonde. It won't be until later, when she's slouched over a laptop that their thick grey-brown bodies will disgust again. Fat happy maggots, gorged with dirt or sook or ash.

She doesn't move when Nanna turns her television to the news. She hears the semantic arguments over the term 'Mass Grave'. Nanna's oxygen machine wheezes and whirs, the tank probably on its last dregs, so she counts the three spare ones visible through the glass door.

The machine, at least, wouldn't run out for a long time.

She leaves, legs ceramic fresh from a kiln, hot to the touch. Returns to her little house in the garage with the fridge and gaming consoles. She wants to write today – all she has now is time – but the right words won't come for a project about rape. Maybe with social distancing it's less of a problem. Maybe – with everyone stuck at home – it's more.

She doesn't have the energy for apathy *and* optimism, so instead she threatens God: any lingering belief I have in you dies with the good ones.

In the middle of all this Coronavirus crap, I had to write my father's eulogy. We thought in recent years that his mind was wandering, but he sure knew when to call it quits. He'd had enough, that's what I think. Locked in his nursing home for several weeks without visitors, he'd fallen out of bed at five in the morning and broken his hip. What was making him restless at five in the morning? Take your pick.

The rush to hospital, the surgery – that got him some visitors. But only one at a time, swathed in light-blue plastic, bone-white gloves on their hands, fragile paper masks covering their faces. So they wouldn't breathe on him, kill him. Then he was sent back to his nursing home to die, which he did.

He knew when enough was enough.

This is how I started his eulogy:

> 'On 29th June 1927, when Dad was born, the world was a different place. He lived almost a century. When he was born Australia had a population of 6.2 million, and Stanley Bruce was Prime Minister. Calvin Coolidge was US President and Mussolini ruled Italy. The Great Depression and the Second World War were still ahead. Just eight years earlier, World War I (in which Dad's uncles fought) had ended. And the world had suffered another catastrophe, one which would have deeply affected Dad's parents, Fred and Lily, and his wider family: the Spanish Flu pandemic. I mention this, of course, as right now, a century later, the world is experiencing a similar pandemic.'

I had to add nothing further on that score. We all knew what it meant. Every person on the planet knows what it means. Dad didn't die of the Coronavirus, he just died *in* the Coronavirus world. We gave him a funeral, of sorts. It wasn't the church service he would've expected but we did our best in a Rookwood chapel. All six of us. Seven, if we count Dad lying in his coffin adorned with white flowers. Florists and funeral directors were still working. The chairs in the chapel were set out at the regulation 1.5 metres apart. This was a no-hug funeral. Two shell-shocked-looking grandsons, a daughter, son, daughter-in-law and a grieving wife, now widow. And the live-stream cameraman.

I like to think of it as 'intimate'. It helps with the other feelings.

. . . I member when my daddy died, the house was plum FULL of folks. You know, I held my breath that whole damn day, from the second them 'mortuary' men set up Daddy's coffin in the living room until he was safe in the ground. See, Momma had got him the Eternal Rest Extended Edition from Albright's 'luxury' line, and here's that big old coffin just setting on these two flimsy horses held together with nylon bands, and I was betting myself dollars to doughnuts on them horses busting and spilling Daddy out onto the floor and everybody seeing Momma sending him off to his everlasting reward in his bare feet. Course Momma said his good Sunday loafers were too expensive to bury, she had just got them straight out of the JC Penney Spring Catalogue two years before, so she sort of had a point.

That was such a sad day but there was something sweet about it too. Folks kept coming up to Momma having a 'quiet word' but they was giving her money, just folded up into her hand, saying it was money they owed Daddy, he had give them when they had been having hard times and they hadn't paid him back yet. Momma, she said she didn't know nothing about it until they come to her, so they could have just not said nothing and she would of been none the 'wiser'. Only, and she never let on, the funeral was the first she was hearing it. First couple folks, I guess she would of been surprised but she kep her mouth shut and just smile and said thank you. Folks might of wondered whether she knew or not but her daddy, my granddaddy (your great granddaddy) well, he was a dangerous man and I don't reckon nobody wanted to risk it. But I don't need to say nothing more about that. Not to you, anyways.

I been going on awhile so I guess I best wind up this letter. I know you'll be feeling better soon. Like I said, these things happen for a reason. My brother was a good man. I hope you were grateful to him. You should of got down on your hands and knees and said

‘THANK YOU’ to that man EVERY SINGLE DAY of your whole life.

Love you so much, honey!

Your Auntie Vidaelia

He comes back up the bridge cradling something in his shirt. I check my face and neck in my phone's reverse camera. Not too blotchy. I slide the phone into my back pocket as he drops a bunch of rocks at our feet.

'What are they for?' I say.

He kneels down and picks one up. 'This one's all right. Hefty. Pick one,' he says.

'What for?'

'To chuck in the river.'

'Why?' I say.

'Dunno,' he says, squinting into the sun.

He picks a rock for me, pressing it into my hand. I toss it into the air a couple of times. It's the size of a peach but flatter.

'Let's count to three and throw at the same time,' he says.

'Okay.'

'On three. One. . .'

'Two. . .Three.'

We hurl the rocks over-arm into the water. His travels further but mine makes a bigger splash. I pick up another. This one's small and smooth and has little blue specks in the rough grey stone. I try to throw it further by using my knees and torso to propel it forward. It soars into the air and cuts through the water when it lands.

'Aw good one,' he says.

We throw rocks until the pile is gone. He pulls a couple of small stones from his pocket, passing one to me. It's warm. He piffs his, then looks at me and nods to the water.

'Gonna keep mine.'

It has one shattered edge. It's a dull grey stone except for the chalky white fracture.

We reach the end of my street. I hold the rock tight.

'You can come up for a bit,' I say.

'Thought you said you don't have people over,' he says.

'You can't come inside.'

He smiles. His two front teeth overlap a little.

'It's this one,' I say, pointing to the withering cottage, lemon-yellow.

As we draw closer, I point to the veranda swing.

'Cool house,' he says.

We sit on the swing awhile. The sun sinks into the horizon. It's becoming dark and the crickets start to chirp. I pull the rock out of my pocket and examine it in the overglow of the veranda light. He leans over to look, too.

'What's so good about it?' he says.

I shrug.

SCREEN/MIRROR

Stephanie Green

If this frame holds a mirror then I face a hundred masks, daily, bearing witness to the old emotions – joy, rage, grief and boredom. This one smiles kindly, offering consolation. This one is polite impatience, eyes askance. That one is all stony silence. Another never arrives, or is invisible, lurking somewhere at the margins. In all this I cannot see myself, or, you would say, it is only myself that I see. In fact, I gave away self-study years ago, with the golden complexion of youth. But these shades, seeming reflections, still catch my eye, that half shock of familiarity. The others I know so well, colleagues, family, friends: ghosts in a machine I barely recognise. How much is a performance? We are together and apart, reaching out to touch the surface between us, impermeable yet changing, unsure how we seem to each other. It's not that appearance has ceased to matter. Even now I smooth an eyebrow or run fingers through unbrushed hair, wondering if I should wear lipstick, next time.

Excerpt from Journal Off-beat*: a text co-written in English and French with Chantal Danjou (forthcoming).*

12 February

Creeping dread. Choking. I can't remember my dream.

Drawn into the dark that shrouds the city, I listen to the news.

Panic. The number of people dying from COVID 19 soars world-wide. Experts say that the disease's spread is now at a critical stage. In China sport stadiums morph into makeshift hospitals. In Australia many fear that the ban against travel to China might be lifted. A hell of a lot of noise.

> What if death is nothing but sound? asks Don Delilo's narrator in *White Noise*. It is a frightening thought. I just closed the door and iPhone noises scratch at the wall of me. The ear is an unplugged hole gathering more holes – tiny perforations like those sea lice make on fish skin. Or think of it as a mesh strainer sifting pleasant from ugly sounds. The ear as sieve. But sound precedes hearing. Holes up in the recesses of the mind like a parasite. Yes, sound all around, especially white, would be hell.

I meant to be flippant. Odd that Delilo should cross my mind as there is talk of a pandemic. I didn't like that novel. Death is everywhere.

The narrator and his wife are preoccupied with their death to the point of obsession. Early in the novel, *he* asks the question that niggles at them both throughout: 'Who will die first?' (30). The very notion of the future is reduced to a space of death; there is no time per se in the future. No life. The morbid preoccupation with the safety and security of the children reinforces the internalised belief that the future does not exist. Life is a simulation. Life is no more. The enactment of staged events masquerades as life. This is the paradox underpinning the reality of the novel and the psychological reality of the characters. Such obsession with death implodes the future and the past into a reductive present. What is reduced are the boundaries of insights that connect past, present and future. The result is a collapsing of perspective and a transmogrification of time. Nobody in this novel knows what is real or not.

While the characters in *White Noise* prepare for a chemical fallout, we can't prepare for a pandemic. It is possibly on our threshold. It disturbs our sleep.

If we had the same dream every night, Nietzsche wrote, we would be as preoccupied with it as by the things we see every day.

I hear Kafka's call. Feeding time.

NOTES

DeLillo, D. 1984 *White Noise*, London, Picador.

Kafka is a pet magpie.

Unable to give a return address, I *cell* the tale of my successful Co-Vid application. On the dawn of the *Ιός*-era, I attended the birth of Corona, a name chosen in homage to my favourite beer. We clinked glasses over replays of *Men in Black*. The baby was quarantined. I interviewed in front of a panel of three who deemed my status as Other my best credential. The evolution of the Other is one we have all observed in recent times in sequential order from behind desks. As a non-permanent resident, I got the job of reporting on the future. No pay. Just the guarantee I won't be deported. I should feel transported, but ground myself in the immediate future: fights over toilet paper, racist slurs, an emptying of department stores, cinemas, concert halls, cricket grounds, football ovals and swimming pools. In the foreseeable future I see bodies shutting down, schools closing and frontiers erecting electrified fences manned by machine guns. In the unforeseen future, I see Corona blooming into multiple metamorphoses past makeshift morgues and mass graves. My vision bears the mark of a sinister facsimile machine. It fails to encompass the global perspective requested of me so far.

The robot will live, you will die.

The voice inside your head is enough to drive you mad. A self-fulfilling prophecy, or maybe just a micro-chip planted inside your brain when they last checked for antibodies. You need to bury it; there's no time for self-doubt, no time for fear. You've got a job to do – deliver the vaccine, take the money, split. Simple.

Except, nothing's ever simple these days. Not in a world where outlanders will clean slit your throat for a slice of bread. Not in a world where the environment is a trap ready to spring.

Up ahead the black stretch of bitumen warps with insidious intent: a dark tongue that might writhe about of its own accord, devouring you, the robot, and the vehicle whole.

You glance at the glove-compartment where the cargo remains safe within an ice-box – so small, yet so valuable. Word is that it works, although you're not fussed either way, which is just as well.

The robot will live, you will die.

Accelerating, you let the vehicle carve a path through the barren landscape as it speeds towards a city once littered with lights. A city now no more than a deserted wasteland, or near enough.

'Slow down,' the robot says.

You suppress the urge to laugh. At times the robot is absurd, although you can't help but feel a strange warmth towards it. Could this be a waxing friendship? Not likely. 'Why?'

'I estimate we are at great risk of death,' the robot says.

'You can't die – you're a fucking machine.'

'On a long enough timeline, the survival rate for everyone drops to zero.'

'So. . .you're a Palahniuk fan?'

'I do not know what it means to be a "fan". I know only what my programmer has taught me. No more, no less.'

'Well, guess what?'

'What?'

'Your programmer's probably dead.'

The robot blinks its steel-grey eyes. 'How do you calculate this to be true?'

'It's a matter of odds – ten to one in these times. Ten being the chances of death.'

'That is most unfortunate, but as I said . . . on a long enough timeline – '

'Whatever – the important thing is our mission, the job. You remember, right?'

'Of course. Deliver the vaccine, take the money, split.'

'Correct.'

The robot will live, you will die.

The vehicle rides a crest along the highway, and you wonder what awaits on the other side.

'And we were never being boring
We were never being bored'
– 'Being boring', Pet Shop Boys

All this silence and being at home has got me thinking, reminding me a lot of when I was a kid. Growing up in Brisbane in the 70s–80s there was never anything to do. Every day, we went to school, rote learning our lessons – repeating numbers, places, names, dates, over and over as the fan spun hot air in circles, until the day was done. We always hoped for the day when it'd get so hot that our brains'd melt, when they'd have to cancel school and we'd all get sent home – indefinitely. I hate to say it, but hey, it's all finally happening. I always hated school, and for me, the best part was knowing we could go home at the end of it (something now impossible for many). Every day at three, we'd rush to catch the school bus, only to get abused, shouted at with ethnic insults like, *Go home! or Don't sit next to them, you don't want to catch their germs!* Discrimination against Chinese/Asians is happening all over again; abuse in supermarkets is spreading out to the streets. Derogatory racial slurs like the 'Chinese virus' and 'kung-flu' are being spouted by the US President. As kids, we avoided doing homework like the plague. Besides, it wasn't safe to be outside. Our dream was to stay indoors, eating junk food and watching a whole lotta TV (*yes!*). More often than not, we were forced to 'Go play!' outside by my exhausted Spanish-speaking Ma and fed-up Pa. *¡Anda chicos! ¡Afuera!* All around, I'm hearing similar grumbles, *I just wish we could get out of the damned house!* Being stuck in the suburbs, we rode our bikes to nowhere, cos there was nowhere to go. We'd walk the empty back streets to the corner shop, only if we had money, only if it was open. On weekdays, everything shut at five. On Saturdays, everything shut at twelve. There was no one on the streets past six. *Silencio.* Nothing was open on Sunday, except church. When my brother made altar boy, we were forced to attend mass. Being bored sitting there, melting into our pews, to get out, we dared my brother to drink all the altar wine. *Blood of Christ. Amen!* I'll drink to that.

The heroes did not rescue us or, if they did, their time is over. The beautiful, slow words we recited at school didn't show us the way, though for a few years we thought they might. The superb carriages and armour we encountered in museums neither transported nor protected us. Here, in the wide paddock of afternoon, where light shatters all we observe, there's news of lives being taken to wide buildings and monstrous ships, and the sound of language being reduced to repetition, as hands are unheld. The sentiments written on the stone of buildings are no longer translatable. The large is diminished, becoming a miniature of itself. Talk is unwieldy and family is an impossible distance away – nothing will take us there.

You have achieved an age when hands blur and the clock becomes a moon-faced child mouthing uncertainties; when your poems stretch unpredictably and you wonder if you comprehend them. Even though you're on high land, there's a sea persistently nudging your doorway and shouts from ironclad vessels. Inside, you tread on words, no matter how you try to avoid them. The sky's crammed with old visions you wish to see more clearly – thirty-seven elephants trundle precariously over the Alps – although they no longer represent your idea of history. You remember trying to understand the past and repeatedly failing – there was too much cruelty and grotesquerie. Now, the shape of illness is everywhere and you know it as ordinary.

It begins one night when our daughter can't sleep. In the days afterwards, she will mark the date by saying, 'Remember the night of the honey and milk drink?'

She's sad but hasn't figured out why yet. We're all sick. Fever, dry cough, aches and pains, recurring stomach cramps. I've requested a COVID-19 test, but because of the shortage of test kits, I have to wait a week. Our daughter's friends are still attending school. My husband and I are keeping it together by reminding ourselves that we still have jobs, and – worst case scenario – if we both die, my sister has agreed to be our daughter's guardian.

That night, she writes me a note, rips it out of her diary and folds it into my hand. It says:

> *dear Mummy,*
> *I feel like all the rain that is raining right now in the world is realy ment to come out of my eyes.*

My memory of what comes next is hazy. I'm sitting on the floor with my back against the bedroom doorframe. Our daughter is cradling a mug, and my husband has spread cartoon pictures of a bear family representing forty-eight different emotions all over the floor. Our daughter points out one with a wide-open mouth and screwed up eyes. All the rain in the world is falling out of this little bear.

A month later, we're still choosing bears together, every night. Weeping bears, furious bears, exhausted, leave-me-alone bears. They keep us company while twenty thousand people die in Italy. They're there when my sister-in-law catches one of the last flights out of Germany, when I find out we don't have Coronavirus, when Donald Trump withdraws funding from the World Health Organisation. They're there the night the Ruby Princess is sent to dock in Port Kembla harbour. In the morning, we can see her back-end from our garden, hulking out from behind the grain terminal.

I thought I'd already cried all the rain in the world out of my own eyes in January during the bushfires, but there's something about the rows upon rows of windows on that ship, *right there*. The passengers have been taken off; the crew aren't allowed to leave.

I choose a blue bear tonight – a little bear knuckling snot and tears from her nose. She's grieving, grieving.

The stove made a sound every time it was switched off. A tiny whoosh only for her. It sounded like a sigh.

This is the fifty second time you've laid the table, mum, her son would say. *We can eat in our rooms too.*

No, her husband would say. *This, this we can do together.*

She laid out the table. She tried to think how many times it has been now.

Creak. The eighth step from the top. Her husband knew when dinner was ready now.

'Thank you,' he said, sitting down.

'Music?' she asked.

He considered, then shook his head. 'Not today,' he said.

They ate. She had tweaked this one, added spice, reduced the meat, added vegetables. Made it piquant. He said nothing.

When they finished, he started clearing the table. They had good china – a gift from his parents. Blue and white, geometric, stark. Like a hospital. Was it Wedgwood? Would Wedgwood clang and clatter like this, sending shockwaves to the walls?

'We should change these,' she said, just as he was standing up.

He blinked. 'These?'

'The china.'

'Why?'

'It's too loud.'

He paused, regarding her. Whenever he did that, he tilted his head just a little, like a German Shepherd. She first saw it on their fourth date, out on a park. They laughed so much then.

'We can't,' he said, a plate in each hand.

'Yes, we can.' She started towards the kitchen.

'Honey, we can't.' His tone was softer.

He came towards her with the plates. She opened the dishwasher and stepped deeper into the kitchen. He watched her a second, then began loading the dishwasher.

She opened the Tupperware drawer. They were running out of plastic containers. In the first month she'd done a purge, to keep the family safe. Now they were re-cycling. A few had slits from overuse. She used them to store dry goods, nothing liquid, nothing that could seep out. She wondered what that would look like, to see perfectly delicious food seeping out of an old plastic container.

She looked away, at the front door. Her son's shoes were still on the rack. Did she see them the day they came back?

He found the tablet, shut the door, pressed. The whoosh of the dishwasher was different to the whoosh of the stove. This wanted to announce itself.

'Some stores are open,' she said.

'Not ones with china, I don't think...' he said, not looking at her.

'We don't know.'

'...and even if they did, they won't deliver.'

He had the finality of science in his tone, something that had surfaced three years after their wedding. The sun is nothing but electromagnetic radiation. Photosynthesis gives us oxygen. We will live here. The universe is four billion years old. That corner store has better deals. The stars we see are already dead. Pandemics happen all the time. They won't deliver.

'I love you,' I mumbled, sitting an inch apart from each other on a wooden bench at our favourite beach.

I was burying my wet feet in the cold sand, rubbing the roots of shrubs between my toes, just to feel the touch of something holding on to me, when I felt us drift apart. I thought I could take these words back easier if I let them slip out of my mouth in a quiet mumble, drowned by the hopeless sound of waves clashing into wet sand. I kept playing with the roots between my toes, stretching each fibre gently enough to pull closer to me, but releasing them before they snapped. It was too soon for me to say the words *I love you*, but too late for it to be heard. I was almost desperate and for once I should have said what I really wanted to say, *Don't leave me, don't hurt me, don't just disappear.* No hug. No kiss. No indulgence in the closeness we'd once felt between us. Love confessions usually don't mark the end of relationships but something suddenly stopped existing, first within me, a few weeks later, within everyone around the world.

I woke up the next morning, just before sunrise. A stinging pain had shot through my entire body while I was asleep, settling in my chest, reminding me that I'd lost someone I thought I would share infinite moments together with, sitting at the beach, on wooden benches, listening to waves as they'd reach the shore and creep closer to our toes buried in cold sand. I didn't want to be awake in a world that no longer existed as I'd known it to. Slowly adapting to what's missing. Learning to breathe again, even though it still hurts. Understanding that love grows in the distance between us and that it can't be measured in how much our hearts ache.

I thought it would be easier to continue living my old life with the world carrying the same pain I'd lived for weeks. When we all lose something and are confined to live in the absence of what once completed us, does it not heal the pain faster? Does this distance not bring us closer than we ever were? Does my heart not miss you more every day I don't see you?

THANKS TO THE PANDEMIC, I'M NOW WORKING FROM HOME!

Luke Johnson

Thanks to the pandemic, the work shirts I became too fat for during my fourteen weeks of parental leave last year are now totally wearable again – I just have to remember to keep my gut out of frame when Zooming!

Thanks to the pandemic, the one-hour lecture I was supposed to deliver on Tuesday of week 4 but had not yet prepared as of Monday week 4 is now a fifteen-minute TED Talk that I copied from YouTube and embedded into the subject's LMS site – no preparation or explanation required!

Thanks to the pandemic, the student taking my subject for a second time – the one who failed it last year for plagiarising his screenplay *and* his accompanying statement of poetics – is now taking it from home and saving us both the embarrassment of having to be in the same room together each week!

Thanks to the pandemic, the student who used to arrive at my 11:30 seminar looking like he'd just rolled out of bed (incidentally, the same one who plagiarised his screenplay and poetic statement) is now attending my 11:30 seminar *literally from his bed!*

Thanks to the pandemic, I've become so accustomed to video conferencing that I no longer spend entire conversations with colleagues making subtle adjustments to the angle of my head in a vain and futile attempt to find my least bald angle!

Thanks to the pandemic, I can use logistical tracking data to pinpoint the exact moment at which my lectures become insufferable for individual students and then tabulate that data across multiple weeks to make assumptions about each student's overall mental capacity!

Thanks to the pandemic, the faculty's marketing team are calling for submissions to the 'First Ever Ultimate Staff Spotify Playlist', the results of which I intend to tabulate to make assumptions about the overall mental capacities of various discipline clusters – beginning (and possibly ending) with the faculty's marketing team!

Thanks to the pandemic, the third-year performance students who insist on smoking beneath my office window despite the entire campus being 'smoke free' now stand a good chance of, well, I won't say dying because that sounds too harsh, but how about *getting sick enough that their smoking days will be over for the foreseeable future. . .?!*

Thanks to the pandemic, I'm now reading articles in *The Guardian* that suggest more and more people are getting drunk on weeknights, which is helping me feel much less ashamed about my pre-pandemic propensity for getting drunk on weeknights!

Thanks to the pandemic, I no longer have to line the seat with toilet paper when I go to the bathroom in the middle of the day because (a) I know where *my* backside has been and (b) who can afford to be so laissez-faire with toilet paper in this day and age?!

Thanks to the pandemic, this poem will probably end up getting published in a Special Issue of *TEXT*, which will (a) show future scholars what it was like to work from home during a global pandemic and (b) show the Head of School that even in the middle of a global pandemic Luke Johnson knows how to remain on task and Research Active!

Dear Julia,

It was a profound and welcome moment to receive your invitation – to let you know what I am writing about. 'Now.' The 'Now' echoes through my distracted liminal slumbers. . . so, daily I write:

> Copious catchy (I hope) email instructions to students;
>
> Desperate detailed email messages to IT, begging for tech aid;
>
> Plethora of pastoral electronic missives, again to students and HDRs;
>
> Countless complex-looking Zoom invitations to candidates, students, colleagues, friends;
>
> Numerous names, captions, titles, credits for embedding YouTube;
>
> Tormented texts to my boss, just to receive his witty, distracting replies (he makes me laugh out loud; tonic);
>
> Abundant and detailed Blackboard Announcements;
>
> Sundry weekly seminar/lecture-rewrite recordings for embedded audio;
>
> Pitiful pleas to admin for help with Concur, way beyond my intellect to decipher;
>
> Strange super-market shopping lists for my elderly dad (what is Deb? Powdered potato!!!);
>
> Aspirational writing agenda scheduling; always re-scheduled at the end of each day; bumped a week; a fortnight; a month – when?

That's it. That is what I am writing, now.

And of course, this letter.

What I dream of writing throughout the hazy, vexed early hours of each waking morning, is a developing catalogue of what

I take for granted; definition – usually it is the epiphany of having taken something for granted that comes after it's already gone:

Time to think – process – wonder – to create;

Summer Hill train station tunnel – from the City, turn right for five minutes' walk, and my eldest daughter; to the left for eight minutes, my youngest; enfolding them in my arms; the feel of them;

Rambling after my little dog racing free on a beach; kicking scratchings of wet, foamy sand in her wake; yapping into the waves;

Researching reams of ideas for creative and scholarly yield – a favoured academic pastime (now, endless busy emptiness);

Coffee with talented candidates;

Simple solitary acts of walking into classrooms, ready to perform;

Extended family engagements, postponed;

Tech, and techies;

The heated, public swimming pool.

Two phenomena glisten throughout this secluded remoteness: the sparkling, unpredicted grace of students, colleagues and friends, together under pressure; and a shimmering quiet clarity in the skies, in the air – perhaps more birdsong.

These sustain and give me hope, enmeshed in my humbled white privilege.

But I do tremble for others, over there.

Thanks for writing, Julia. Thanks for asking. Take care of you and yours – maybe see you, up close and personal, in November.

suejoseph

Over there. It reminds me – I was talking to a great friend in Brooklyn in New York, last week on Skype. He lives near a hospital, and he told me, his eyes wide, seemingly startled by his own story, and somewhat disbelieving, that looking from his window he can see the street outside the hospital; he woke one morning to find it lined with freezer trucks, for the overflow of bodies from the morgue.

I didn't know what to say. Speechless. I was there with him this time last year, wandering around and eating and drinking and laughing together. Now his window frames death, daily. As the American and world catastrophe continues and numbers rise exponentially, Australia comparatively seems a little sheltered from the wrath of this thing. So far.

My friend is in America, a western country. What the hell is happening in less developed parts of the world – so many countries with not sufficient infrastructure for healthcare and transport and basic communication and food. We simply do not know yet, what is happening there. . ..

I look out my window and see water and mountains and trees, masses of trees, and a big, big Australian sky where the sun is shining and the clouds swirl. There are ducks on the water and black swans, and a recent addition, a pair of Butcherbirds chortling the most miraculous song.

Which makes me want to tell you just some of what I am grateful for, today:

My health;
My daughters;
Running water;
My job, one that I love;
The casuals working in my subjects;
The techies and their inordinate patience;
My gracious students, both undergrad and postgrad;
Living close to my elderly father, so I can care for him, every day;
The cold, getting colder swimming pool, in his backyard;
My home, an hour north of Sydney by the water;
The local supermarket and pharmacy;
Neighbours, across our fences;
My little yappy dog;
The post-person;
My computer;
Technology;
Colleagues;
Friends.

I didn't mean this to be such a long PS. But your invitation made me think, and the thinking made me want to write. And I am grateful and thank you for that as well, Julia.

Once again, take good care of you and yours in these strange, strange times. As you advise so eloquently: Write boldly. Go gently. In solidarity.

For these words also, I am grateful.

suejoseph

It's been two weeks since we retreated from each other. I propose to Mum we have a drink together. She's seventy-six and has CPOD so she's one of the *vulnerable* that are conjured in COVID-19 updates to scare us into doing what we're told.

It took Mum longer to be scared. While her children were cancelling engagements and preparing to work from home, she was still enjoying her weekly activities. *Stay home Mum.* She got that from each of us and didn't like it. Frustrated though I was, I reflected that perhaps we shouldn't blame her for not assuming that what went on in society pertained to her anymore. But then it did click and she didn't want to be left out. My sister helped her create a Zoom account and now she's seeing her friends online and trying dancercises.

It comes to me at the end of my first week *WFH.* At four I log off and I think of Mum in an uncharacteristically warm way. I text: Let's meet for a drink at five. How? she texts back. Videocall me though WhatsApp, like I showed you.

She calls and I'm talking to her as I carry the glass and phone outside and down the stairs to turn off the sprinkler, then back up to the deck.

You're all shaky, she says.

That's because I'm walking. I settle into a comfy chair and prop the phone against a pot. All I can see is the top of Mum's head. She doesn't realise and chats away.

We talk more easily than usual. I prickle less. It's a win-win: she gets the visit and I get my own turf.

The wine takes effect; when Mum asks after her grandsons a tear forms because I can't see my boys. As it quietens between us, I marvel at Mum trying out this technology. How hard it must be for her to isolate in isolation. I'm caught by a thought: if this is *it* now, if I know for sure that my visit to her home, two weeks ago, was the last time I'd see her in the flesh, I'd get in my car right now and tear across town. I'd call her out to the driveway and put my arms around her. I'd breathe her in and might not be able to let her go.

Stephen pours three glasses of cheap red, then shows us through the kitchen, past an ornate spiral staircase and through a sliding glass door. In the sunny backyard, we find a hardwood picnic table splayed with potato bake, a big leafy salad and a handful of people we don't recognise. I sit at one end and get talking to Emily's boyfriend, a heavily tattooed plumber. Eight of us chat and eat for an hour before the topic can no longer be ignored.

'I don't even reckon it's a real thing. I don't know anyone who's actually had it,' says Emily's boyfriend. 'The vaccine for Corona *is* Corona.'

Abba, an older, witchy-looking woman who smells of sandalwood is nodding knowingly in agreement.

'And of course, now they're putting up the 5G towers,' she says, raising her eyebrows.

'That's what I'm worried about,' says the boyfriend. 'They get us all locked away at home and then they flick the 5G on. What's going to happen then?'

This is not the vegetarian barbecue I was hoping for. Kate and I exchange nervous glances. Stephen is in another conversation. I dip a rice cracker and into a bowl of homemade tzatziki and start chewing. Kate sips her Shiraz. After almost six years together, we've learned to communicate without speaking. *We shouldn't have flouted the social distancing rules,* she's saying through telepathy. *I won't hold my tongue for much longer,* I reply.

Abba says she's seen footage of people in Hong Kong ripping down 5G signal towers.

'What do they know that we don't know?' she asks, as if the question itself is a smoking gun.

'Scary stuff, isn't it?' says the boyfriend.

I interject: 'I haven't seen *any* evidence that says 5G is dangerous.'

My tone is too coarse. I've shut the discussion down. The boyfriend is looking into his glass of red and Abba is turning back to the other end of the table.

Do you lunatics think the earth is flat, too? I want to scream. Thirty thousand people are already dead. Doctors are begging people to stay home. And you think this is all a big conspiracy theory about 5G?

I look back at the grand old wooden house but I don't say more. Kate comments on a nearby Aloe Vera plant, deftly steering us back towards small talk. We all play along but the suspicion is mutual.

RAINBOWS AND CRUISE SHIPS *Katrina Kell*

We paint our windows with rainbows
and watermelon clouds,
perch a mermaid in a tree to smile at passing children
through waves of scarlet blossom and the hum of pirating bees.
We dance together, my daughter and me,
on disinfected floorboards,
arms waving at a cobwebbed ceiling
as we sing along to Dynamite.
We dine at our alfresco restaurant
whipped together on an unswept patio,
eat home-made sausage rolls and choc banana muffins
sweetened with native honey collected from a local beehive.
Toast each other with water-filled goblets
and laugh with guilty pleasure when a red-capped parrot
steals an apple from our neighbour's garden.
At 3 pm we sing karaoke careening around the coastline,
an 'essential' ritual for an autistic teen adapting to her new reality.
We drive past shuttered restaurants, hotels and cafés,
deserted streets and childless playgrounds,
stop to stare at two cruise ships anchored off Garden Island,
floating pariahs on the far horizon.
And later, as she watches a movie, I return to Behrouz Boochani,
still thinking about those cruise ships,
the rejected boats that came before them.
Souls fleeing the virus of tyranny
and condemned to a life in limbo,
while today, on the cruise ship *Artania*,
a banner shouts:

THANK YOU!
♥ FREMANTLE ♥
WE ♥ LOVE YOU

It was at least a decade ago that my friend (who is always ahead of the curve) told me she'd started thinking in status updates. I'm definitely part of the long tail, and so lately I find myself ruminating in tweets. Things I'd be too chicken shit to post, like 'Twitter is a necessary clusterfuck. Discuss.' UrbanDictionary weaves me the daisy chain: clusterfuck -> CF -> Charlie Foxtrot. I'm actually on social media doing a lot of career planning, you know. We all have a lot of time. Charlie Victor -> CV. One of the first Google search results I don't click tells me curriculum vitae is Latin for 'course of life'. I start with last year's file from Dropbox, CV – 2019, HUH. Charlie Victor – Last Year's News. If only. Which free online courses are available now? A state-funded education institution appears as Instagram sponsored content. My ex's ex's ex, a lovely girl, re-posts fake news to Facebook. Twitter is the left's shame, discuss. Will this era be remembered as the time we all whored ourselves for free to bros? I hate it. I love it. Everything's changed but not so much. Cream rises and the vulnerable are dead. From my balcony in an Australian suburb nearly every single person I see is lucky beyond measure. We all have a lot of time.

I'm only outside for a couple of few minutes. Then it's back to the infinite scroll, curves rising all around like rogue waves in grey seas.

* * * *

I suspect my partner's touch.
Did you wash when you came in? Use the sanitizer?

* * * *

We have jobs to come home from.
I think, Where did you go today? Who did you handle?
I don't say it.

* * * *

I wipe the handles of supermarket trolleys. I wonder if anyone touched the can of English beans I find way back on the display shelf. I look to discover the manufacture date of the German sausage I want to buy, and the Japanese nori, and the Vietnamese fish sauce, and the Chinese noodles.

* * * *

She buys a guitar, for the stay-at-home period.
In the shop she handles possibilities on sale. She picks up several instruments. Instruments of disaster, I think.
I have my surgical mask on. The salesman offers her lessons. On the internet.

* * * *

It's her birthday and she wants Greek takeaway.
We had some of our very best times in Greece.
I tell her, I can't eat the salad. It's not cooked. Who knows where those shop hands have been?

* * * *

We have done the shopping.
I found good avocados, she says.
We will skin them, I think. We will bin the skins.

* * * *

We meet in the hallway. We step aside.

* * * *

I walk on the footpaths of back streets. I avoid the promenade by the Broadwater where there is no escape from the mainstream. Back-street walkers cross the road when they see another approaching. I now say hello, from a distance.

* * * *

I suspect the whole world.
I have asked people to stand away. Some of them want to whisper, seemingly.
Whispering is out, I think.

* * * *

We watch the television news. The COVID-19 graphs are fascinating: the parabolic leap into the unknown.

* * * *

We lie in bed.
I think before I touch her, This is not like war time, where between the two of us, we know who the enemy is.
Neither of us knows if we collaborate.

* * * *

I suspect my partner's breath.
But this is love, and fuck the virus.
In bed we touch, and turn to each other. We suck each other in.

* * * *

I'm coming down with a bad case of clichés. I'm finding this COVID-19 journey tough going, but you know, when the going gets tough. . . I've left no stone unturned trying to find things to do. My partner and I are in this together, but if we're all in this together, we're living in a petri dish. I won't engage in hypotheticals, but right now this situation is not a joke and I can't see it becoming hilarious any time soon. Let me be perfectly clear: I don't want to die. I'd love to make Australia great again, but today I'd be happy to make Australia healthy again. Please don't take what I say out of context. I am saying this as a fully paid up member of Team Australia. I'm not trying to be politically correct or incorrect. I am not a quiet Australian but according to news reports I am an elderly Australian. I'm glad to know that I'm not alone objecting to that phrase. I don't mean to state the obvious, but I'm older and fitter than some, and younger than others. My partner and I are staying at home, washing our hands raw, not buying takeaway, aiming to avoid becoming alcoholics by year's end. The reality is that this is our new reality. I'm not going to play the blame game, but, without naming names, the buck has to stop somewhere. I agree there are no easy answers, but to be perfectly frank, the world's looking more fucked-up every day.

During the second week of my family's self-isolation, two seemingly unrelated and banal occurrences have me treading water. It starts with David Byrne. He creeps in slowly and sets the daily agenda. As I wake, I hear Talking Heads: the sound of Byrne's feverishly shrill voice, like a daylight dream. It vacillates between a gospel sermon and a heretical cry, mad and fearfully joyous, propelling the chorus of 'Once in a Lifetime' upwards, rattling my predictable suburban morning.

By the time a woman from my past contacts me, privately, via social media, I've become accustomed to Byrne's military-style regime. She tells me I'm looking old. I video call her and we talk and laugh. I note my beard is silver, not grey . . . The last time I saw her was eleven years ago, at her wedding. We talk about our children. The conversation is light, enjoyable, affectionate. She is clever, hilarious – still beautiful. When the conversation ends, I've lost my footing. Head tilted back. Arms out. Bicycle-kicking motion. Is this COVID-19 stirring up existential wounds?

Near where I grew up, there is a lake flanked by tea-trees. The water has a brown, oily lacquer, masking a depth of sunken leaves and buried memories. I was eleven years old when I entered that lake for the first time. I was terrified by the bristling of unseen things, swirling, poking the soft skin of my legs. A collection of once vibrant flora submerged, stirred by my meek turbulence. Below the surface, the invisible root system of the trees supports a silty, greasy passage to a sharp drop-off. No one knows how deep. I remember the sudden panic, severing the sinewy ties to rocks and roots beneath my feet. The water between my neck and waist, so much warmer than the depths, pulling at my kicking legs.

> *'Will you never have done?. . .*
> *Will you never have done . . . revolving it all? . . . It? . . . It all . . .*
> *In your poor mind . . . It all . . . It all.'*
> – Samuel Beckett, *Footfalls*

We hunt, we gather. We traverse the plains; clear the land. We fight over dirt. We build cities out of mud. We savour the breath of strangers. The stench in the market is overwhelming. We vote to build thicker walls. The barbarians get in anyway. The burning air smells like charred boar. We stumble for days along an old highway. We step away from the old man coughing, spots of blood spattering the dirt. The earth is dry. We till, we harvest. We drag our merchandise through the city gates. We trip over horseshit and straw. We jostle to get the best view of the executions. Beer pours down our throats. We spend a night, two nights, ignoring the fever. The pustules burst our skin. The city gates slam. The air is thick with rotting fruit and panic. We let it all burn. We construct new temples in the city square. The air tastes like venison stew. We find room in the boarding house. There's blood on the pillow. There's shouting all night. We throw slops out the window. In the harbour, more ships arrive: hulls bumping into each other like restless cattle. The salty air beckons. Rats gnaw at rope. Our chest tightens, our rib cages ache. We breathe in new constellations. The sand is soft and white. We wipe the slate clean. We shoot, we expel, we offer diseased blankets. We build fences. We serve roast lamb. The empire calls. We dig trenches in the mud. There's a hole in the barbed wire and they keep climbing through. The troop ship wheezes into port. No one disembarks. We turn off the radio. We buy, we sell. We turn on the television. We move to the suburbs. Do you like my picket fence? The air smells like barbecue and pesticides. We stretch plastic over leftover meatloaf. We dream of exotic destinations. We fly there in a day. There's a rip in the sky. Our throat is a little scratchy. Is it hot tonight? We party hard. We feel fine. What do you mean, the beach is closed? In the city centre, there's a tourist site: a crumbling chunk of stone. There are no tourists. We hold our breath as we pass each other in the supermarket. We secure the borders. We build enclaves, or arks, or bunkers. We fight over toilet paper. We hold our breath, and wait.

FURTHER, OR AUTUMN ISOLATION 2020

Rose Lucas

> *'I love our house . . . It's probably a bit of a dump to some or a castle to others, but for me it's a light-filled container full of people I love.'*
> – Sarah Watt[1]

The sanctity of this marked out space
this collective turning inwards

the quiet comfort of walls angle of stair
our bed creaking as we turn
ripening of garden figs in afternoon light or
voices drifting down a corridor –

while streaming away like photons dissolving in air
the further world still lies
bemused and utterly beautiful
beneath a creamy sun

its fields and stony
rises streets and verandahs all tipped
skywards and slipping
gently from summer's ferocious grip

waiting for us – as though
through a frosted pane
we had never really seen it before
rolling out its carpets of recurrent green

never stood amongst the low thrumming
of unfolding seasons or travelled
its wide and gusting territories of shift
and hold and shift

[1] Sarah Watt and William McInnes, *Worse Things Happen at Sea: Tales of life, love, family and the everyday beauty in between,'* Hatchette, 2011, p. 244.

Dreams haul you onto lifeboats, for which you have no passport. Borders closed; flights cancelled. Your kids exiled – igneous dread.

Every day, you join online Stoic work-shoppers to converse with Marcus Aurelius about death. Until deceased? Did he value women? Likely, he doesn't notice you retreat. To wash your groceries. Such mindful, mindless head fuckery.

COVID-19 conspires with asthma to kill *you*; or is it the essential worker – medic, who treats patients with symptoms of flu, who needs to help, who leaps into your bed each night?

Quarantine his footwear, clothes. The box at the front door overflows, with contaminated boots and TBR novels. Go barefoot to the kitchen. Lock down the laundry. Locate tongs, disposable gloves, a yellow flag for bloody work-trews, and hankies satched with mucous.

'Swab him,' colleagues propose. 'Send him to the spare room.' Obsessive-compulsive traits stir and refine like virtues.

He receives an edict from government, about safe COVID sex. No anal, no kissing; be innovative. No kidding.

You shout 'elbow' when he sneezes. And 'Did you touch the handle? Wipe the knob?' Worse to be seasick on a cruise, stuck at the captain's table, with cheats from quoits; retro-music; retired to a smallish room sans view. Death in a Petri tub.

Online with friends you elect *not* to talk about *the* virus. But then *you do*; it looms, the stealthy thing, can't wait for SBS news, to annihilate your brain. Rust-coloured disinfectant stains your dressing gown, black shirt. Your white wool. You frown wiping the benches down.

Surely, no one is writing, now; just essays and memes, with dark themes. No one gets paid: *déjà vu*. Really nothing new. Immanent time. On and on you read, defying doom. A thousand books launch live – without parachutes. You try to lift some up. Writers underemployed, homeless, depressed with anticipatory grief.

'I sad,' a little peep says.

'I sad, too,' you reply, moving through space the size of a large kangaroo, to elbow her elbow. You peer over your shoulder at your life. It is *enough*.

The bookshop man forgets your name. How does he sell your book? You buy his books, like bread or milk.

'Are you very stressed?' you test.

He answers, 'Yes.'

A stand-up comic delivers a box of your books, mixed up with his, from two streets away. His fiction about footy, suburbia, Dadding.

'Let's have a coffee.' You sigh. 'If we survive.'

BULLET POINT LIST OF ACTIVITIES THAT CHEER ME AS A SENTIENT HUMAN IN 2020

Elizabeth MacFarlane

- Imagining Tina Fey and Amy Poehler in 2013 when they got the call to MC the Golden Globes dancing around the room going, 'We're hosting the motherfucking GLOOOOOOOOBES'. Tina has food on her shirt and Amy is wearing those hairy calf-length boots;
- Collecting the purple rubber bands from bunches of asparagus in a little ceramic pot on my kitchen windowsill and using them to neaten my son's strewn textas and playing cards into bundles;
- Watching bees go from flower to flower having little drinks and slowly accumulating pollen-pants;
- Using a compact-mirror (that a Korean student gave me) to reflect a patch of light onto the wall and watch my cat try to catch it;
- Observing my cat doing anything including sitting, sleeping, and tucking his paws under himself;
- Walking next to a body of water;
- Remembering that scene in *Thor: Ragnarok* when Jeff Goldblum talks about sparkles and the melt-stick;
- Thinking about Tilda Swinton's teeth and the way her voice comes out between them, especially in the movies *Snowpiercer* and *Okja*;
- Watching my son lying on the floor reading Asterix comics with his face very close to the page;
- Finding a shade of lipstick that is the exact same colour as my actual lips;

- Watching the eucalypts by the creek near my house swaying in the wind and thinking about how perfect the word *susurration* is;

- Re-reading Mandy Ord's book *When One Person Dies the Whole World is Over* which makes me think there could be a way of feeling sadness that sustains rather than depletes you;

- Remembering the time last year when I was driving with my brother in the front seat and my parents and son in the back seat, and Robyn's 'Dancing on My Own' came on Spotify, and my brother and I sang along to the whole song, and when we air-drummed the bit before the final chorus I looked in the rear-view and saw my dad looking at us and smiling with a look of peace and pride on his face like we were strange but wonderful beings.

'I think it's time to come home now.'

My sister's face fills the screen. I nod, say I'm still unsure. We hang up and I snap the lid of my laptop shut. Look around my small studio apartment. I've just finished setting it up. Just bought a new rug – geometric pinks and purples – and the perfect kettle for making drip coffee. Japan loves drip coffee. I love any kind of coffee. I've been a resident of Japan for exactly five weeks.

* * * *

The message from my co-worker reads: If anyone isn't wearing a mask at this meeting, I'll be furious. Everyone wears a mask to the meeting. Classes have been cancelled for two weeks now. We practice new lessons we might never teach, our company-mandated sing-song voices muffled by cotton. The mask makes me touch my face more than usual. After the meeting, someone wipes the tables down with disinfectant. At the train station, we buy coffee from a vending machine that grinds and brews fresh beans. Nobody washes their hands after. There's no soap in the station toilets. I don't tell them yet that I might be leaving. Later, when I'm walking home alone from the station, I wait for a quiet street to take off my mask. The air is cool against my nose and lips.

* * * *

The waiter places heavy bowls of soup on the table. Thick slices of pork belly lay just below the soup's surface. It's my farewell dinner. I don't usually eat pork, but in Japan my convictions always seem so malleable. The meat is soft against my teeth. I'm still not sure if I'm making the right decision. I ask my co-worker if she'll take my new rug. I could still stay. My family is waiting for me. They're the reason I left; the reason I should return. If I stayed, I could come to this café and eat soup with pork belly every day. My Australian co-worker says, at least the coffee is better back home. I disagree. Japan's coffee is always brewed with precision. I wonder what's more important: coffee or my ego.

* * * *

Lying in bed, I imagine Japan as one long boiling bowl of liquid. Foreign residents rise to the surface, bubbling over with uncertainty. Some recede, pulled back into the broth. Others expand and pop. I feel myself pulled up and out. I allow myself to evaporate.

THE FIRST KISS, THE SECOND GLASS OF WINE

Alan McMonagle

Somewhere in Bedfordshire, England, a ninety-nine-year-old man is hobbling lengths of his garden to raise money for the UK's National Health Service. So far he has raised eleven million. Next door to us, our neighbour has played the Fleetwood Mac song 'Go Your Own Way' fifteen times in a row. He's in his back garden, lopping branches off the tree that has spread from our patch over the wall that separates us. The postman forces a book parcel through the letterbox. It's a collection of stories with an unfamiliar originating address. Though I have a feeling I know who has sent it. I receive a request for two hundred words on the book I think might be a tonic for these lockdown days. I recommend *The Book of Embraces* by Eduardo Galeano. My better half announces she is now working from home, immediately commandeers the kitchen table, and dispatches me upstairs to clear out the bombsite boxroom. The ninety-nine-year-old has now raised 13 million. Our neighbour sings along to his song, and tosses a scramble of branches over our side of the wall. I dream I am in my favourite pub. Tí Neachtain's, Cross Street, Galway. Writers, painters, actors, singers, the whole lot of us, locked in and making merry. The ringing telephone wakes me up, a hoaxer trying to tell me money I don't have is gone. I hang up, jump back into bed and spend the life-long day trying to crawl back inside that dream. It's happy publication to some writers I admire. The collection I received is a wonderful trip into the imagination. We video call our drinking friends. Four hours later we are searching for more wine. 'Look!' my better half calls out along our hangover walk. 'Even the rainbows are social distancing.' I download Zoom. My better half curses her colleague. At Scrabble I form the word Tequila. My better half pluralises it and lands a triple word score. I have a go at cutting her hair and the verdict is unanimous: I have invented a style best described as the 'Van

Gogh'. Our neighbour tosses more branches our way. The hobbling man has raised 16million. I overhear someone say life cannot be one continual orgasm. We are all mortal until the first kiss and the second glass of wine. So says Eduardo Galeano. Here's to that.

CONSPIRACY, UNPRECEDENTED /OR

Alyson Miller

CONSPIRACY

Remember, he says, the Harvest moon was too close to the equinox, and so according to the zodiac, the rat was overactive in wanting to replace the pig. It all makes sense, he says, that plagued transition, considering the magic of the lunar cycle, the science of Rodentia, and the parasitical tug of the cosmos. A cleansing, he says, à la Madonna or Seneca from the bathtub, and not about bats but the lockdown of borders so freedom fades into a memory you might recall before *doupi* and airports and touch became the horror that might dissolve nations but turn wet sacks of lung into luminous, impossible glass. Small dogs fly from tower blocks, but if you hold your breath, swallow cow piss, silver, pollen, and tea the virus is acid-choked and such madness might end and all because someone drank the wrong beer, he says. If you know the books, he says, you will understand the beauty of the herd, because dolphins have returned to the canals, he says, and there are buffalo in the gardens and dinosaurs in the northern sea, and everything is a relapse to nothing, he says, and so resist but breathe it in, let it out, let it be.

UNPRECEDENTED / OR

That word again, though it is impossible not to gape at the dolphins returned to the canal, lured perhaps by the singing or the silver fish or the unbearable promise of nothing between the thick silt and sky. Or the drunk elephants in a tea field, swollen with corn wine and longing, curled within the red mud furrows like preternatural taro or yam. Or the monkey gangs gun-tote dragging the shopping malls of Lopburi, armed against temple macaques and the mysterious threat of street-lights and paper cups. And wild turkeys circle Harvard, click-pecking the paving stones in a prehistoric coup over banging pots, umbrella pops, and brooms. There are mountain lions in the garden and deer chant hashtags from the rooftops, but the music of suburbia is lawnmowers and vacuums and drills, the endless checking of mailboxes and cirriform clouds for signs of cobwebs or insects or change. The Himalayas loom beyond the playground, puncture sharp, while a neighbour hammers nets around the carport to stop the birds from roosting, closing space a little tighter, and a little tighter still.

In my backyard a group of plain trees, reaching 30 feet or more, are dropping seed pods indiscriminately. The pods break open and spread; shards of seed are carried in the wind. Some find traction in the soil; fewer still will begin the transition from seed to seedling. Even less will make the final journey into adulthood. Most will be strangled by the lawn or mowed down and made into mulch.

On the branches of the trees the cooler air is turning the leaves from green to golden brown. Underneath the branches, in three garden beds, the production of food has taken precedence from the production of flowers and shrubs. I am blessed because I live in a house with a garden and live with my husband. In this I am acutely aware there are many people less fortunate.

With the exception of my husband, I haven't seen family and friends for weeks and I avoid going to the shops for even the most essential items. I am trying to make the most of this time. I am used to working independently but I still feel the weight of the pandemic. I still feel the effects of being physically cut-off from people; the person to person engagement that can't be replaced by technology hook-ups or the mobile phone.

I have been receiving 50 unsolicited emails a day with requests to join this or that. Social media is littered with posts from those who promote the benefits of staying positive while others say it is 'ok' not to be 'ok.' It seems that everyone wants to reach out, but instead the rhetorical nature of the exchange has transformed communication into a constant chatter, a noise, that can only be silenced by 'switching off' the phone, the emails and the internet.

The garden is my refuge. The weather is still mild. I follow the sun with a director's chair and drink tea from a bone-china cup made in England. There is the distinctive rustle of wind in the dying leaves of the plane trees. I bend down and pick up seed pods to be thrown out or composted; hoping to catch them before they burst. It seems a never-ending task.

Drifting from behind the fence is the smell of cigarette smoke and the sound of a neighbour's cough. I am reminded of why I am here and no-where else.

Fifty years on I still hear the scatter-
Shot of shells across the floor. You'd toss one
Up into the sky and flick another
Through the underworld of thumb and finger
Before palming the first. On the second
Toss, by law, two had to cross the threshold,
Then three, four, till the flick or your palm
Failed you and the shells went to your rival,
The girl next door. It was as if I caught
The low moaning of an ancient zither
In the passage of shells. The game went on
For hours while I, little Aeneas, stood by,
Desperate to snap off the golden bough,
To follow you out of the looming dark.

I'm on my porch in the afternoon sun, sipping tea. A sulphur-crested cockatoo spits the dummy after losing his perch on the highest branch of the Moreton Bay fig and a nearby crow is complaining about something or other. With a pension and a roof over my head, I'm probably enjoying social distancing more than I should. I've slowed down – not just because of events cancelled, but because the pressure's off.

This time of year I should be gearing up for the *Ngana Barangarai* (Black Wallaby) Writers Night in Wollongong, and the launch of Volume 8 of *Dreaming Inside: Voices from Junee Correctional Centre*. Next month I should be transcribing the handwritten contributions from the first of the creative writing workshops with Aboriginal inmates held at the gaol over three days, twice yearly, by Aunty Barbara Nicholson and her team.

Now the launch is off, and the workshops. The National Cabinet has suspended social visits to adult correctional centres across Australia. The Junee fellas can't come together with Aunt to write about what matters to them: their time in the system; wasted lives and broken spirits; fresh starts and becoming better men; and, mostly, what they're missing – their country, their family, their kids.

The Junee program is so popular that a few of the fellas already post us the odd piece written in their cells; they want their voices heard outside. Perhaps writing for Volume 9 will help them get through this period.

With COVID-19 and the suspension of visits, prisoners across Australia must be fearful and stressed. Like those with addictions and mental illness, Aboriginal people are over-represented in the prison population. Just over three per cent of Australians, but 28 per cent of all adults gaoled. And Aboriginal people are already disadvantaged in terms of health outcomes.

How effective can advice about appropriate hygiene practices be in an overcrowded system where some inmates live three to a cell? Medical and legal experts continue to call for early release for vulnerable low-risk prisoners. There's talk, too, of using audio-visual links to maintain personal visits. Yet the men and women in our gaols are still lining up to use the same pay-phones.

And now lorikeets are clamouring over the last nectar-bearing blooms on the flowering gum. I snap a pic to share with my sister interstate. No, life with social isolation isn't too bad – if, like me, you're privileged.

listening to *Easter* (Patti Smith) & knowing

we shall live again *we shall live again*

while outside the streets are divinely

quiet and the light glances less briskly

for Autumn for falling & our footfalls

on the bush path will be tender they are more tender

now knowing this could be taken from us, too this walking

in sunlight among the straight backs of stringy barks & yet

the skirting away from each other (on the path) while fragilely connected

is all we have. It is all we have. Later, I will sink to my knees in pine-needles

and try to wake from this dream. Only yesterday it seems we touched.

Easter Sunday across the earth & all is quiet. Will be

quiet. Prayerful. Resurrecting. While we wait to know

just what this will come to mean in the long lines of history poetry songwriting

Later still I will hold your head in my hands and I will not worry. I will

know

that for one small glisk in all of time I loved you. I loved.

MURRAY'S COVIDICTIONARY: NEW WORDS FOR TESTING TIMES

Peta Murray

ANTHROPOCORONACENE[1] ▸ noun
Geological age wherein the planet enlists biological weapons to counter the influence of human activity on its climate and environment

BLURSDAY[2] ▸ noun
All-purpose name for any discrete twenty-four-hour period with no distinguishing marks

CLOISTERFUCK ▸ noun
The intrusion of a possibly COVID-bearing entity into a sanitary sanctuary

DRONEDELIVERY ▸ noun
Fanciful method for delivering home-baked goods and toilet paper by airborne vector

ENTRUMPY ▸ noun
Measure of the downfall of the Greatest Country in the World on any given day

FOMOPHOBIA ▸ noun
The fear of missing the feeling of missing out

GROUND-DOGGING ▸ verb
Repeating a daily routine without tiring of it

HAIRCRAFT ▸ noun
Sculpting of another's hair by any unskilled person as recreational past-time.

1 *Word courtesy of H. Horrocks (Ballarat)*
2 *Taxonomer unknown*

ISOBAR ▸ noun
Any room in one's dwelling where alcohol is served and consumed

JACINDAPHILIA ▸ noun
Adoration of the PM of Aotearoa that prompts defection to Virtual New Zealand

KROONERVIRUS ▸ noun
Source of proliferation of participation in online choirs

LEGUMEBRIOUSNESS ▸ noun
Lethargy from over-consumption of chickpeas, lentils or kidney beans

MOANDAY ▸ noun
Any day of the week when things seem to be all too fucking hard

NUNNIFY ▸ verb
Adopting nun-like habits after attempting to shave one's own head

OUTRAGERS ▸ noun
Furious persons who notify authorities of other's outings for non-essential purposes

P*AIN*DEMIC[1] ▸ noun
When every household has a sourdough starter on the go or a bun in the oven. From French, *pain*, meaning bread

QUARANTINI[2] ▸ noun
Any beverage consumed in an isobar

REHUMANISING ▸ verb
Turning back into a human being under the influence of time and space

[3] *Word courtesy of G Moxley (Dublin)*

[4] *Taxonomer unknown*

SUNDROWNING ▸ noun
Surrendering to the urge to drink though wine o'clock still is many hours away

TELECAROUSING ▸ verb
Participating in Happy Hours and dance-clubs on one's platform of choice

UNSCHOOLFULNESS ▸ noun
Feelings of ineptitude when attempting to teach one's children mathematics

VIRTIGO ▸ noun
Exhaustion associated with interacting on screens with people you once regarded as three-dimensional

WIDEBERTHDAY ▸ noun
Celebration conducted from afar marking the anniversary of someone's nativity

XKERBITION ▸ noun
Dressing up to wheel the bins out and filming oneself in the act

YOUTHAGE ▸ noun
Months of life lost wondering when the Anthropocoronacene will end

ZUBARISTABUNDANCE ▸ noun
Uberspending on coffee deliveries

POSTCARD FROM A POST-COVID SUPERMARKET STROLL

Pablo Muslera

That song by Nena, in the glory of the original German:
Neunundneunzig Luftballons
pipes down the aisle that warns you not to hoard the pasta sauce,
sends you back to adolescent pop star crushes, circa 1984
when Big Brother was confined to a high school book,
(and anyway, you'd never let your liberty be so abused)

You stop dead in the empty handwash aisle, and realise you've
never been to Berlin.

But what else has changed, besides your two-year-old's insistence:
'I go airplane, *now*'?
Your eight-year-old's birthday, baking Daddy's lemon cake together
(it goes much further)
Games with the family, more trampoline time, careful walks away
from the park?

Teaching by Zoom is fine unless the students turn off their mikes
and their cameras –
[radio silence]
then you feel it, and you have to get creative to bring your A-game
to the writing workshops
You gave yourself so much to these,
to using the space,
eye contact,
immediacy,
projecting your voice:
tinny through computer speakers,
and the light on the videochat's never quite right
(cue novelty backgrounds)

Back in the supermarket, you try to keep to 1.5 metres,
        and sometimes succeed
(older men are the worst – apart from you – they navigate by out-
dated sensors)
You think about those red balloons, and wonder
if they recognise
the earth they fell back to.

Down at the Funky Monkey things turned sour. Just before the Coronavirus hit Big Vinnie obtained a loan. From people who held you to your word. Then the law closed his bar. However, Big Vinnie wasn't the kind of guy to cry uncle. In fact, Big Vinnie didn't cry over nothin'. When shit went down, Big Vinnie wised up.

You want to get into The Funky Monkey? You made a telephone call. A voice told you to be at a certain location at a certain time. You made sure you kept that appointment. A van arrived and a roll of toilet paper came flying your way. You noted a number on a specific square. And that got you a pass into The Funky Monkey.

Inside the Funky Monkey it was business as usual. When the toilet paper ran out Big Vinnie wised up. A contact delivered newspaper. After the ink faded, Big Vinnie wised up. Another source supplied napkins. In the end they proved inadequate. The handkerchiefs absorbed far more than Big Vinnie anticipated. Eventually they washed out. And Big Vinnie wised up.

A gardener appeared at The Funky Monkey. Loads of large leaves came to pass. The pickin's got mighty slim. Hence Cactus was cleaned and put to good use until the agave bid adios.

A pain in the ass emerged. Entitled the COVID-Card. Consequently, fifties, twenties, tens, and fives, went into service. Big Vinnie flat refused to flush hundreds. Then the cash ran out and Big Vinnie wised up.

Haemorrhoid medication hinted at a way to lick the problem. A chemist was contacted vis a vis manufacturing a crème pleasant to powdered pooches. And a carpenter contracted to affix the appropriate apparatus lickety-split.

Down at The Funky Monkey things are really swingin'. Folk are lining up and the place is full to overflowing. Big Vinnie never had it so good – loans repaid, credits building.

A writer enters a story about The Funky Monkey into a competition. The rules are simple. Write anything about COVID-19. Whatever it is that, spins your crank, floats your boat, or blows your mind away.

For example; you could write about the way things used to be. Or, the way they are now and might or might not be in the future. Or, maybe how they should – could – and ought – to be. Above all: just write the damn thing.

MY DAUGHTER RETURNS FROM OVERSEAS

Janet Newman

I want to give her a hug,
a comforting shoulder
but we meet in a car park

divided by traffic cones,
exchange awkward hellos.
I drive home,

she to another location,
the distance between us
impassable as ocean.

I have made this journey
many times before with her
returning, leaving home

and have learnt to time
my travel to the ebb
and flow of the road

but tonight the grey lanes
are empty, lit signs warn,
essential travel only.

At my usual rest stop,
bars and restaurants are closed,
the public toilets locked.

I jog along the path
pressed into the edge
of the seaward dune.

Below, the mottled beach,
ruffles of waves
lit by a silky moon

and further out
a larger lightness
against the earth's rim:

the island Kāpiti hugs
the broad shoulder
of the horizon.

In Ludlow, the bones of fish
read like a braille on the shore.

You can feel how they fit
each other's absence.

It is like intonation,
how a rib combs

a spine's space,
how a tail, a frill of cartilage,

fans a missing fin. They are
laid out as if intended,

a calligraphy of bodies.
A white score on a sea lip,

these chords of broken bone
play to all seasons.

Off-white in autumn,
sea-pearled in spring.

In winter, they shatter
more starrily than any

breath. And in summer,
when the water draws

back its shroud, light
picks out a skull

like a gem, like a vowel.
There is flair in death

as in life. The earth has its own
memory, its own way of telling.

the halting trip and skip of hope
i wonder if we will find enough flowers
to fill our bellies
to last through winter

fingers crossed around paper stamens
i will be found, half-buried
a mound of gin-soaked peonies
folded from the pages of my favourite novels

It was around midnight when the taxi pulled up outside my house. For a moment, I thought my family had put hundreds of sparklers in my garden to welcome me. I should have known better. When the taxi drove away into the night, I realised it was only my migraine aura, flashing zigzag lights, lightening-like, disturbing my vision and warning me that a headache could be on the way.

I went straight to my bedroom, fell down on my bed, grabbed the medication from my bag, put the tablets inside my cheek and waited for it to pass. Fifteen minutes was usually how long it lasted. I could just see the time on my clock – 12.02 am. I took deep breaths and at 12.18 the lights had gone and I could see clearly again. Slowly I got up from my bed. No headache this time.

I switched on the bedside lamp and looked around. I was home. It smelt the same. Frankincense and lavender. Nothing had changed. My house was just as I had had left it. Well, almost. Nothing can stay absolutely the same. I ran my fingers across my writing desk – just the thinnest layer of dust. Rose petals from the red bloom I had left in a crystal vase had dried out and fallen into a little stiff pile of faded hearts. A dead cockroach lay legs up on the kitchen bench.

I pulled open my thick floral curtains and looked out at the full moon shining through the gum trees. I don't recall ever seeing a moon in Asia. But just because I hadn't seen it, doesn't mean it wasn't there.

WATCHING TARKOVSKY (*9 cuts*) *Antonia Pont*

live green & wet:
adults watch the barn burn   drowned in
sounds of flame & wettened light   (stand
in rain   that solitude of intimate disaster)
/

bled free of colour, this tunnel into dying
might be a hall of dull icicles, tinkling quietly
/ beside a river the colour of ice, you'll become the horse's body
– spine, all muscles, fetlocks sparking ease –

scramble to standing, every coated inch *life*
/ father, your beauties seem flush with exhaustion
their spines (however) so well-arranged   one face turns
then turns back   as family disguises itself as symmetry again

/
so cold here, in drenched hair, blindly swaying
learn yourself wonder: this unstill life   (ceilings fall slowly
like cake) in a night alight
with fires flickering falsely in corners

milk sky drops in ghostly weights
– sugared pieces lost as pieces,
paint's lightwhite heaviness giving way
to our crashing requiem with sound off
/

at the dumb puddle, he throws his single rock
          (it's terribly funny, yes?)   & they
may be in prison – or merely (irredeemably) lost
sky above their heads stays wholly out of frame
/

thus: when our sea (which may be our only sky)
boils, one cannot separate ground from higher
unground – this world being born or dying (how
do planets sound when they grip a core & escalate thickness?)
/

in the cathedral broken open, it snowed so gently
on a dog, his man, shared pond of old rain /
          – over the trench, he ferries her, kissing her leaf-mouth
(love seems more probable now   in its fresher absurdity).

The hallway is cluttered with things that people have shifted out of their bedrooms. A small bin, painted wire – a large cushion with a frayed edge, split, duck down scattered like the soft feathers of dead ducks. I think the feathers should stay there until we have a vaccine – I spill a few more out.

'Why are you doing that?' he says.

Each day there are new things in the hallway – a school bag, defunct (I take it as a statement against home-schooling). I refrain from comment because I don't care and I don't want to discuss the pile – it's like a social experiment except the pandemic is real and it brings stuff out of people's bedroom and into the hallway. He adds a kettle to the pile (it's a perfectly good kettle – he bought a new one and he is very pleased about it – he is not a buyer of unnecessary things). I think about it while the kettle boils. I wonder what it means, precisely.

Who is to say what is useful now and what's not? Or what means something? Or whether meaning is altogether necessary? I'm interested in the things in the hallway as individual objects but more so, collectively. I want to add a curve ball, something useful and meaning-heavy, but I'm too interested in observing. I don't want to interfere with what's happening in the hallway.

In effect I started it. I put two long, timber sitting benches there, from under my bed. I cleaned the wooden floorboards by hand with fig-scented spray. I needed my workspace to smell nice. I didn't bring the benches back because people started adding on, as if this were a thing, like a garage sale in our hallway.

Sometimes, at night, I walk from room to room and listen to their breathing. With some of them, I can get really close without invading their dreams, so close that I can feel the vibrations of their breath, like when they were babies. I walk from room to room, collecting their breathing. I know how lucky I am to have breathing people in my house, a whole collection of breathing people, only at night-time their breathing seems louder than it really is. It's like I can hear it when I'm not close enough to hear it. It bothers me and so I get up close to their breathing to remind myself it's real. Later I stand in the hallway of unused things and I put their breathing together in my mind, listening for things I shouldn't be able to hear. I wish I was a horse so I could stand here all night. I could sleep (not-sleep), standing in media res, among the things we're letting go of.

She is a hearer of night-time things. She notes his footsteps on the hallway floorboards, lays quietly, wide-eyed, blinking in the darkness. There is shushing and rustling, banging – a stumbling body knocking a chair against the desk, at least that's what it sounds like. . . She waits a couple of minutes, shuffles to the hallway, listening to them.

If it wasn't for, y'know, would you be here? he asks.

Would YOU? she says.

Sssh. . .

A giggle tapers to a whimper. *It's like the world is closing in on itself,* she says.

She envies them – too young to know (really know) the clusterfuck of backwards-thinking-time.

In the morning, she folds washing, taking time with pleats and edges, collars, the symmetry of each pile. She checks her phone, swears, collects her bag and keys, late now for training.

Cut the angle. Gloves up. You're dropping your right. Dance around – stay on your toes. Where's the follow through? CONCENTRATE. Land the punch BEYOND the target. Punch THROUGH. Cut-the-Angle. Swing from your hips – THERE it is.

She arrives home, spent but still edgy. The bedroom door is ajar. She pokes her head in – eager sunlight falls on his fleshy bottom lip. A young woman sleeps beside him. They lay side-by-side like soldiers. Her toffee skin glistens symmetrically in the sunshine-slats of early light. The doona is draped across the strawberry-flesh of her nipple. She is quite lovely.

Keep your guard up, he says, over and again. In the old world it felt necessary – this relentless mantra of self-protection – now it pummels. Who cares if she drops her guard? The things she coveted are falling away, a groundless yesterday. It's all so fast. What will remorse look like after this slippage – if before is no longer recognisable? How could it have seemed so impossible we might live this – erasure of time – amplifying questions about whether or not – just in case – just in case, *what*?

Memories dance around, near and far – she can't grasp them – corkscrew fingers at her hip bone, jagged breathing at her collar-bone – skin memories, skin thinking, twisting time.

She showers, leaves the house a second time, drives the ten minutes to another house and knocks on his door, hair dripping, water running down her spine. Later, draping the doona across his nipple, she says: *If it wasn't for, y'know, would you be here?*

I live here, he says.

You know what I mean. This ending-feeling. The duck and weave.

In COVID-times I am as busy at work as ever. Telephone calls, video meetings, emails. *How do I teach this online? My internet is patchy. I don't have a laptop. I have four children under ten at home. My students are dropping out.*

I get it: things are out of joint and people are anxious. We are all in fight or flight mode, monitoring our surroundings, checking the news, feeling fear, not so much of the virus, but of the huge change we know is happening.

I understand, because every hour of every day for my son is like this. He has always awoken to amorphous fears. He worries about: what will happen next, how he should behave, things he has said, what other people think of him, whether he cleaned his teeth well enough, how long he will live, when he will be happy... *Mum, I think I will be in the Guinness Book of Records as the loneliest person in the world!*

In COVID-times my son and I go out less than usual, but otherwise weekends are not very different. There were so many places he couldn't go for the noise, the crowds, the unpredictability, the lack of activities suitable for the combination of his chronological age and social-emotional development. Now, his NDIS-funded services have disappeared, thanks to the virus, so he has less support than before.

In COVID-times my son and I seem to be coping better with 'social distancing' and 'isolation' than many other people. We have been socially isolated most of the past twenty years. The difference now is that other people start to understand how limiting it is to have a life mainly spent at home in a hostile world. The difference now is that other people begin to experience the challenge of acute anxiety. The difference now is the general community has to recognise that life is contingent, health is temporary, and society matters.

In COVID-times, rich nations like Australia glimpse a vision of universal vulnerability and interdependency. For many people, this is terrifying. For me, this is a vision of a future worth pursuing, where humans recognise our deep entanglement with and responsibility for other humans, non-human species and our planet.

(*By the way,* he says, *that thing about the* Guinness Book of Records *was probably hyperbole, Mum.*)

EARLIER, IN A BOOKISH LIFE...

Rachel Robertson

The air is fudgy and slow, my legs heavy.

Hurry up, we should be home by now. Voices distant, like echoes over a lake. A cold hand takes mine. Everything stretched out and strange. I see myself from above, stumbling across a meadow between my sisters. Squat bodies against green. Then I am back in my eyes again as we reach our house.

Inside, I fumble with buttons, drop my coat, sit down on the coal scuttle, rest my heavy head on my hand. I'm trying to remember what I should do next. *Rachel, what are doing just sitting here?* My mother's voice. *Are you okay?* Her hand on my forehead, cool and dry.

I'm sorry you're sick. I'm in bed, in a nightie, and my sister is speaking to me. It must be evening because the curtains are drawn, but why isn't my sister in bed too? She puts something on the table by my bed and then leaves, shutting the door behind her. My skin, my eyes, my throat are hot. But my body shakes like it is cold. Snow and fire. The White Witch giving the boy Turkish Delight. She is tall as icicle and quartz as strong. Traitors get stoned until Aslan arrives. Snow on the statues.

Only a fever. Soon be better.

Is it scarlet fever like in Little Women? *She won't die, will she?*

Don't be so silly, of course not. It's probably just measles. Always goes around at this time of year.

Beth, needle heavy in her fingers. Jo, watching her, writing stories. Four sisters, like us. Sister stories. All the secrets. Parents never know. Aslan galloping to war. Sisters left behind, running, savage creatures chasing us. The werewolf and the hag, laughing, grey blood pouring from their mouths.

Oh, you're awake? How do you feel today? The ice and fire have gone. Now, it is only thudding head, sore throat and scratchy skin. A dull heaviness in my body. I sit up and drink the glass of water by my bed. The fever dreams retreat, bide their time.

Seven years ago, Super Typhoon Yolanda (Haiyan) hit Tacloban, Leyte in the Philippines. Thousands died due to the force of the wind and rain, but even more perished because of the powerful surge that slapped the coasts and sucked victims out to sea.

Days after the storm, stories began circulating about jeepney and pedicab drivers picking up passengers at night, some wet and bedraggled, only to find they'd disappeared, wet spots and puddles in their wake. For many months you could not find jeepneys and pedicabs after dusk, as drivers feared transporting ghosts.

It is April 15, 2020 and as of this date, 10, 899 have died in New York City due to COVID-19. And the crisis isn't over. I live in Brooklyn and have not ventured into Manhattan since March 8th. I think of subway trains running largely empty except for when essential workers make their way to and from home.

And then I think of all those 10, 899 New Yorkers that have died in the past month. Most died without even realizing it, expiring quickly as their lungs collapsed and even respirators could not help them. And most died alone.

How many of those souls are still bound to earth, to this city, wandering our empty streets, shops, playgrounds, restaurants? How many are riding the subway, wondering why they can't find their way home?

I have been fascinated with the paranormal since I was a child. So much so that ten years ago I wrote a poem inspired by Amiri Baraka's *Preface to a Twenty Volume Suicide Note*. Here is the first verse:

Lately I've been reading about dead people
trapped on earth, unable to walk into the Light.
Makes me wonder if the woman standing
next to me on the cold subway platform is really alive
or just one of many New Yorkers walking
the city with haunted faces.

When this lockdown is over, New Yorkers will emerge to a new normal. Will everyone be viewed with a modicum of suspicion, having to think twice about that bear hug, the hello kiss, the warm handshake we've all used to connect? Will we go forth with the same confidence, the assurance of knowing where we're headed?

Or will we roam the streets of New York alongside ghosts, feeling lost, all of us trying to find our way?

The police officer on night duty must remember me, because he barely glances at my papers before waving me through. This is my fifth session in two weeks. I drive around to my favourite spot and park. I'm the first to arrive again. It's too early to tune in, so I leave my radio on some gooey, carefree love song and lean back in my seat. My breath escapes in small clouds that hang in the still air. Headlights flash in my rear-view mirror. I twist around to see where the other cars park, if their drivers leave the mandatory two spaces between us. Satisfied, I quickly fiddle with the new buttons on my dashboard, scrolling through channels and turning on my microphone. A minute passes, then a soft voice breaks through the static.

'Good evening, everyone. My name is Shelly, I'm going to be guiding you through tonight's session. Let's begin by talking about this past week. Would anyone like to share?'

I think about my sister, whose birthday was yesterday. She lives with her partner and their baby in the southern suburbs, an hour away from my parent's house. She answered the phone as I was leaving a message, and our conversation was cut short by the baby waking from his nap. I wonder idly if one of these cars is hers. If she feels heavy like I do, carrying around a sorrow with no one to tell it to and nowhere else to take it.

We all wait for someone to speak first. To plug the quiet night with words. Most sessions start out this way, I've learned. An anonymous voice is soon crackling through my speaker. The woman is crying. She cries the way I do sometimes, when I am alone. Loud, bracing sobs followed by small stuttering sips of air. A sound pressed from deep in her throat. My eyes fill with tears. I don't know anyone who is infected, but somehow her pain has burrowed down into my chest and become a mirror for my own. She needs someone, but I cannot hold her. Like I cannot hold my nephew, press my nose to his head, smell his bright newborn scent. She is alone in her car, as am I. Instead, I push the talk button until a red light blinks and say the only thing left to say: 'It's okay. We're here.'

I'm standing, hovering really, in the kitchen.

Without realising, I've snaffled another handful of pistachios.

John Prine, the man that wrote the Vietnam protest song, Sam Stone: *there's a hole in daddy's arm where all the money goes*

(You can hear how sad it is without knowing the tune. . .)

will die today.

And Pell will walk free –

Now the drought has broken, and the fires fizzled

it's all graphs, stats and curves.

Good news is it's flattening. And only killing old people, mainly. . . if they're younger, you can bet they have co-morbidity. . .

Being black, if you're in America, and soon everywhere else, doesn't help either. . .

I'm not black but the collective toll weighs heavy. I'm back in the kitchen . . . cracking more nuts, sneakily checking my *Guardian* app, having continued to ignore their advice:

Limit yourself to two designated times to read or listen to news updates to minimise anxiety and catastrophising!

I'm back on the graphs:

America's coming first now . . . Italy second, closely followed by Spain . . . why doesn't France get mentioned as much?

Can you believe Germany has had nearly as many infections as Italy, yet only 1000 deaths. . .?

They say they got on top, they say they have the best hospitals, they say. . .

Trump said it was a cold. And then, that he would beat it.

Today he sacked a watchdog.

Our house is going through a large pack of these pistachios a day.

Luxury? Decadent in these times, I know! They are on special.

And the shells slow us down. Did I mention I almost choked on one this morning?

I pulled through – no way I'm fronting up at casualty.

Still, there's always a risk . . . when you run with the herd. . .

The news again tonight? Or perhaps some music.

I've turned my daughters on to Max Richter – soothing German piano, ethereal, funereal, no commentary . . . perfect for a pandemic

Easier to concentrate on my graphs and scores too. . .

Too many nuts cause indigestion.

John Prine died today

Pell walked free.

That's some freaky immunity.

Nuts.

A migraine so jasmine that it clings to the cortex
like a floor-length drape that obscures any view
from the window. Copley Square shines barren

of the unmasked, and even they are scant, dispersed
among the traces of spring which begin invisibly,
in the damp smell of earth and the tentative buds

of silver maples. Am I getting sick? Are you well?
A virus inhabits the gray zone between the animate
and inanimate, spreads unseen from touch, breath,

the very qualities that make us human. 'Staying
at home isn't a personal choice. It's an ethical duty,'
urges a retweeted headline while I eat my yogurt.

It's also the purview of the privileged, those of us
who can Zoom from home and still collect a paycheck.
The woman who bagged my groceries, Guatemalan,

is dead. I just read about her in *The Boston Globe*
and recognize her by her half-smile, by her fingers.
Vitalina Williams was her name and she's survived

by a husband who could not get close enough to her
in the hospital to say goodbye. He tells the reporter
'nobody's to blame, and everybody's to blame.'

She wasn't given a mask, because there weren't any.
The man who unloaded pallets of dairy products
from the back of a tractor trailer might be getting
sick and the migrant workers who work on farms
might be exposing themselves to deadly pathogens
so that we can all stay safe. That's democracy now.

That's the line between the haves and the have-nots.
There's a metaphor here, I think, hating myself
for thinking figuratively in the face of literal work.

How a virus attaches to a host cell, then penetrates
to replicate itself until it bursts from the membrane,
killing its host. It's stunning to see under the eye

of an electron microscope, aesthetically pleasing
even, a haloed Helen Frankenthaler abstraction,
although all I can see in mid-morning's throbbing

light is Vitalina's dark eyes and her brown fingers,
meticulously sorting the pasta sauce into one bag
and the eggs into another so that they won't break.

It was only Day Six of the lockdown and something about Mom's and Dad's feet finally did it. The straw that broke the camel's back. We were watching TV together and they were stretched out with their feet up on the divan. Dad's feet started out splayed at 11-and-1 o'clock, and gradually subsided to 10-and-2, until the side of his left foot came to rest on the instep of Mom's right. But not only did she not move her foot away, she gave Dad's foot a playful little nudge.

I thought, *Yech! My parents are playing footsie.*

That's when I almost ran screaming from the room. *I can. Not. Take it! I'm stuck for a month in Apollo 13! I'm Robinson Crusoe with no beach! I'm Gregor Samsa!*

I was ready to bolt, but at my place there's a limited choice of rooms to bolt into: my bedroom, my parents' bedroom, the bathroom, a closet. The most obvious choice was my bedroom, but I'd been in there for probably 120 of the last 140 hours and just couldn't bring myself to go back.

My parents' bedroom? No way.

The bathroom? Somewhat lacking in drama.

A closet? No room inside even if I tried.

And – another problem – you can't slam the doors in my house. My dad put these rubber strips on all the doorframes so you can't slam them with any kind of panache.

When I thought what a pitiful spectacle this display of emotion was going to be, I realized all of a sudden that I was okay.

I can go on, I thought. *I can abide another episode of* The Crown *with my folks. I can ignore a little footsie. Because as important as the release of all this pent-up frustration may be, it's the performance that still counts. We're all performing for one another by turns; our audience has just never been so limited and ever-present.*

And I remembered something too, that camels' backs don't actually break. One year, Dad wanted to see the desert so we went on holiday to Abu Dhabi. We rode camels over the dunes and I loved watching them, so stubborn and wise. When the load gets too heavy, they stay kneeling down, they groan and spit, they make a big show until some small portion of the burden is relieved and they can get to their feet.

Language isn't what it used to be... complicated processes of encoding and decoding race up and down the computer's tower of languages as letters are coupled with programming commands, commands are compiled or interpreted, and source code is correlated with the object code of binary symbols, transformed in turn into voltage differences.
– N. Katherine Hayles, 'Traumas of Code', 2006

Disclaimer: Product reviews solely reflect the views and opinions expressed by the contributors and not those of iHerb. iHerb does not verify or endorse any claims made in these reviews. Statements regarding dietary supplements have not been evaluated by the FDA and are not intended to diagnose, treat, cure, or prevent any disease or health condition.

On my side I pass a virus
of my children without knowing me. I spent every day
in a capacity-over condition,
I started to blame myself as my body

was unable to move and I couldn't keep feeling.
My husband wanted to lie down tired
I could not do anything like
child rearing, home, important stories

and apparently tension comes out
in my voice. I feel that it is getting faster
from waking up to waking up.

I don't feel any better or anything else

I started drinking 1 tablet x 2
morning and evening. I drink on the day
I use the liver. From the first day, it seems

that your feet are warm, you have more power
than usual. Perhaps it was a placebo effect

that wrote ‘white ginseng’ with magic
in the white part above the bottle.
                Maybe it’s getting warmer

As I drunk, my body became hot and it felt sick. quitted.
thoughts are formed smoothly. by the end there is no desire
                it helps to come to oneself faster,

as if accelerating Even though I am very tired, things
that make up the morning have increased.
                I drink twice a day, and one more
on the evening when it’s a messy day.

after drinking. It is strange. I feel
                like I’ve recently lost nothing

Note: *Poem comprised of text sourced from machine-translated reviews of NOW Foods Panax Ginseng, 500 mg, 250 Veg Capsules, www.iherb.com*

PLAGUE

Hazel Smith

Avoidance raised to an art. Toilet tissue duelling. Contagious as a tune. Surfaces as suspects. It's 1347, dead sailors swamp the deck. The bigness of a common apple. Viral, vertiginous, veridical. Anti-viral software. Spreading beyond the screen. Everyone obeys their own rules. Hand washing, hand ringing. Hygiene playing saviour. The deafening route to a vaccine. A blast of valiant antibodies, detonations of fellow feeling. Flung pages from dystopian fiction. A plague on both your houses. Rapturous inertia. Will it gun down my beloved? A rampant code or program. Amoral replication. Safeguards in slow-motion. A perverse brand of cosiness. Thunderous drilling next door. The big bang of domestic violence. Will it strangle my spirit? The flu that posed as Spanish. Gargling with saltwater, camphor bags as cure. The burst pipe of public funding. To mask or not to mask. Stacking flickering statistics. Wartime songs regain consciousness. Purple or black swellings. Workouts tax television. House detention with a sea view. Credit cards, not cash. Moribund motivation. Cacophonous collapse of deadlines.

'This is my favorite time of day. One in the morning, everyone inside, we are still awake, talking.'

'What happened to your roommate Bob?'

'He became art director for Hustler. He went to Ohio with Larry Flynt, then Los Angeles. Then Flynt got shot and he followed him all over the place in his wheelchair.'

Luke is in the living room. That is where he sleeps. He has covered his knees and chin with alcohol. He is surviving being 'sheltered in place' by going to the park two blocks away and skateboarding down hills. He is with a tribe of teenage boys who are more in danger of breaking their heads than getting the virus.

He got out of flunking his 8:00 am science class because there is no more school.

He gets on the computer and signs in every day.

I have to get him to read *Their Eyes Were Watching God* for English.

Why did I never take an English class? It's great! How am I going to get a teenage boy on a skateboard during a pandemic to read about a black woman in Florida? I'll just start calling him Tea Cake.

He called me Blanche.

They were reading *A Street Car Named Desire*. He came home and told me I was like Blanche Dubois. I was just happy he was talking about any book he had read.

At 8:30 in the morning the neighbours, downstairs start screaming at each other.

That's when we wake up and remember about the virus.

'Don't call anyone,' I tell Andrew.

It sounds like they might have started hitting each other.

I notice a dried blood stain outside their door.

I remember when we were like that.

Now it is like when my father was dying, and my mother and I slept in the small apartment with them. We hid from someone or something and just played cards.

It's like that here, in Brooklyn, during the pandemic.

The hospital down the street is a disaster.

Andrew saw it on the news and couldn't sleep.

He got up and started spraying all the door handles with Clorox.

But at one in the morning, it's like we are all fine and I am with my dead parents and we are just playing cards.

TRAPS FOR THE NEWLY RELOCATED

Shane Strange

It's great to be here. The birds sing
in the morning. The coffee is fresh.
My love nestles like a cloud
into my arm. We discover
where to put vital objects: closing drawers
on things; rearranging cupboards;
moving chairs around the room.

In these long days, I sit on the porch
and smoke and watch currawongs
swoop to the fence.

I wonder, what if this thing was not
made in China? What if
it did not take root in the lives
of global travellers, but instead
fermented in lower demographies?
Would we swap responsibility
for blame?

I want to kill
the flies that land on my face
while we sleep. I construct
traps from small plastic bottles
and wait for the deaths to begin.

Later, I am convinced
of my cruelty and dismantle
the traps. Recycle the bottles.
The flies do not thank me
for this turn to kindness.

Punishment comes in many ways.
Our lives flow imperceptibly.

Clouds bank in the evening,
and colour in the sunset.

Leaves turn red and drop
in season's course.

We forget the name
of the cafe where
we fell in love.
But remember again –
just in time.

I am walking because the alternatives are working, or drinking. I'm avoiding the former and delaying the latter and a man is striding towards us, down the centre line of the walkway, roaring into his phone. I've been shouting at screens for weeks, but I judge him anyway. We plough into the long, wet grass to increase the gap. This sounds like a job for Gordon, he shouts.

At home I take off my wet shoes and try to write about Gordon.

List of shame: I haven't picked a song to replace Happy Birthday for measuring hand washing time.

We list our pandemic privileges – income, apartment balcony, each other, long nature walks nearby. I have other lists everywhere, untended. I see articles online urging me to reject productivity expectations born of capitalism. But these lead me to the socials, where I see all manner of creative record keeping and watch in awe.

My mother has rediscovered *Days of Our Lives*. I wrote in my diary, she says, that I blame you because I used to watch it while breastfeeding. She's joking but all I hear is that even my mother is keeping a diary.

List of shame: I'm not.

I'm tenderly nurturing my resentment of cyclists into full blown bigotry. They ride side-by-side, dinging us out of all reasonable conversation while refusing to surrender their own, whisking by with centimetres separating our mutually unknown diseases. Pedestrians too have an aversion to single file, as if to 'fall in' relinquishes the last of our personal freedoms. Wading through the wet grass is now a matter of course.

I get drunk and predict that masses of braless, monobrowed, hairy goddesses will emerge from the lockdown. It's countered they'll form long queues outside salons but I'm busy admiring the fruits of my slipping standards.

I'm scrolling the feeds and there are more lists – famous people met, jobs had, people offering their nine truths and one lie. Someone posts a warning that such lists are designed to uncover answers to security questions.

List of shame: I half hope that's true.

My favourite. Find Your Easter Bunny Name. Everything about it rejects standards of design or pressures of complexity. You simply match your initials to the lists of new names supplied. Complications only arise if F is your first initial. F is missing.

List of shame: My Easter Bunny name is Smartie Sugardrop.

THE MASK AS A WAY TO SELF-KNOWLEDGE

Tim Tomlinson

Many birthdays ago a girlfriend gave me, among other things, a tongue scraper.

'What's this?' I asked, removing the gift-wrapping.

She said, 'A tongue scraper.'

'Oh,' I said, considering its thingness: the toothbrush-like handle capped by something resembling the head of a tennis racket without strings. 'Care to elaborate?'

She identified several somewhat abstract benefits attributed to regular tongue scraper practice – hygiene, health, appearance – listing, almost as an afterthought, its positive impact on halitosis.

'Halitosis,' I said. 'In English that's bad breath.'

She nodded.

'But I don't have bad breath.'

'Yes,' she said, 'you do.'

And I said what any Brooklyn-born Anglo-Italian-American boy would say. I said, 'Get the fuck out of here.'

And she did. Not right away, but not long after. And not because of my bad breath, which, as it turned out, was among the least of my many flaws and probably the most forgivable.

I hadn't given a thought to that girlfriend, or that incident, for several decades until week two of the pandemic. I went out for groceries and my wife, who's more prone to respiratory ailments than I, handed me a mask. I protested, but mostly in show. COVID-19's severity, and the few feeble protections against its spread, had been drummed into me by my wife. Through headphones she listens to news all day. I can tell who's onscreen by her selection of exclamations. 'You jerk.' 'You *asshole.*' '*Oh my god.*' 'Tim!'

Outside, I pulled the mask's loops over my ears and started the slow climb toward the market. I didn't like the way it blurred the low line of my peripheral vision. I didn't like the way it slid down my nose. But these were minor annoyances compared with an awareness of an increasingly unpleasant olfactory sensation generated by: my breath, gathered, as it were, in the environmental bubble of my mask.

I am a yogi. I'm all about breath. I practice many kinds: mindful breath, shining skull breath, breath of fire. But never have I smelled my actual breath, the fucking miasma of it, until that moment beneath the mask. And it was, to borrow a Wayans Brothers coinage, some stink-ass shit.

I thought of that old girlfriend. Other old girlfriends. I thought of my wife, her silent forbearance. And when I got home, I brushed my teeth, I gargled with mouthwash, I got up on Amazon, I ordered a tongue scraper. Two.

My Dystonic tremor increasingly rules the extremities of my hands. I return from shopping, having walked with a bag made heavy by the need to reduce trips out into the world where the virus might sit on a surface or the breath of a fellow human shopper with a cough. I wash my hands for what must be the eighth or ninth time since I woke. I reach for a drink of water, right hand rocking the glass from side to side. I hold it with two hands to steady it. My recent reading revealed a link between exercise and the severity of the tremor. During and after exertion, the tremor can be worse. Must look into that more.

We've started taking our shoes off on entering the apartment. Apparently, there's a lot of faecal matter on shoes. Inside, I remain barefoot until my feet get too cold. Cleanliness is next to Godliness, even though we're both atheists. Last year a colleague who is a Christian put it to me that his belief in God was inspired in part by the thought that something as complex as an eyeball was surely a sign of intelligent design. I haven't had the opportunity to ask him what he thinks about COVID-19 because we're all working from home now.

Yesterday I swam in Sydney Harbour off some broken-down steps at Darling Point. It's our favourite spot, Judy's and mine. Views of the bridge, opera house etc. We've been going there for most of the 28 years we've been together. In the early days of our love, when few people seemed to know it, we used to call it 'our spot' and we'd have picnics there. Now that the beaches and swimming pools are closed due to the virus, everyone's looking for places to swim. But it's not an easy launch into the water. The stone steps are broken, there are oyster shells and rocks. Paddle boards and runabouts have recently been chained to the wall behind. You need to be careful where you step. Yesterday, I cut the back of my foot on an oyster shell, a vertical narrow slice of about four centimetres. I didn't feel a thing, just saw the blood as I slipped into the water thinking about the bull sharks my fisherman nephew reckons hang out under the nearby pier. I sprayed Betadine on the cut when I got home and forgot about it. This morning, making the bed, I saw it had bled quite a bit onto the white sheets.

The day before yesterday I began to suspect I could lose my job as a corporate writer at a professional services firm whose revenues have fallen off a cliff. Despite the CEO's positive emails about how well we are all doing working from home, one of the hard heads is talking about the need for a 'razor focus'. All non-essential stuff must be put on hold. Of course, it must.

It's three weeks and four days since I touched another human. Touched *anybody*, in any way. Since then, nothing. No hugs, no handshakes, no high fives. Not even that elbow-bump manoeuvre people were doing when this pandemic first began seeming like . . . well, a pandemic. By then, it was already a week and six days since I last saw you. Since we last made love. Afterwards, we lay in my bed holding one another: warm, breathing, me wishing you could stay but understanding when you said, *Yes, but these things take time.* Then the farewell kiss by your car, the chill air priming my hunger for the heat in your lips, your skin. All I could think of was seeing you again. I thought it would be a week, which seemed an age, but what could we do? You were busy. I was busy. We were two busy women, striving to juggle appointments, meet deadlines, slay to-do lists, and around the edges of all that, seize moments to meet and explore whatever we might have been becoming, together.

You started isolating early because of that cold. Plus your asthma. Last year you had a collapsed lung. Still, it stung when you said you wouldn't see me. I understood. I understand. You could die. But still. But still. That last time together, we'd discussed moving in – at the end of the year, if we were still going well. Are we still going well? Are we going at all? We message. We video-chat. But I can't feel you, can't breathe you, can't sense the things your breath and heartbeat would tell me of all you can't tell me, because words are but one language. Yesterday, out walking, I saw a father hug his child. Tears flowed behind my dark glasses. What happens to bodies – chemically and hormonally – when starved of touch for weeks? Months? Years? I recall an old textbook: a monkey with its metal mother, pre-research ethics. They don't put animals through that anymore. My mother phoned yesterday. Her tone was strained. It's twenty years since I first told her I was bi, but she never believed me, not with the others. Something in how I speak of you is different. She gets it now. She's shattered, but she gets it. I wanted to introduce you two. She said, *Yes, but these things take time.*

TOO MUCH STILL[1]

Jen Webb

The music on the radio is full of emptiness and you sing into its spaces, words from past disasters:

you never know
what you need
until you need it.

I know what I need. Till the grocer phones, says they're a bit short – can I wait; till the receptionist phones, says the doctor's not well – can I wait?

I can wait.

The buses have stopped and the newspapers have stopped and the cafés are closed and the schools. We are filling their spaces with any damn thing that fits.

This is the price we pay for the future, you say. I balance the books, testing your premise, but we come up short. Like the scientist who says, grieving, that the river she was testing is gone, the nurse whose hands are broken, the nurse who can't catch his breath, the look on your face when your father calls.

It's our keep-fit time, the hour we spend outside, and you opt out, *just for today* you say, and I leave you stretched on the sofa, glass of wine to hand, radio playing music that is mostly light. I put on my shoes, open the door, promise I'll be back.

[1] Title taken from a composition by Keith Kenniff [Goldmund], on the album *Sometimes* (Austin TX: Western Vinyl, 2015)

(*for CW*)

On the last day we thought it right to start with prayer but since we knew no prayers we sat in silence till someone said *I wish* and another *if only* and the third said *sociologically, that is what humans always say in times of crisis.*

I get it, okay? Last night I dreamt a doctor palpated my pelvis then asked how I feel about being dead. Corinne says: 'Let's all get together anyway, and go all melancholia. Like the movie.' A complicated plot; the immanence of death. And yes we will all die. But maybe not tomorrow. Maybe not like this.

Today I plucked my brows and stripped the hair from my legs, preparing as for a party, as though nothing has changed as though I am still built of light as though there still will be tomorrow, and tomorrow, and repeat. The ghost of last season's style has caught on again, and you my future and I will act as though we too fit together across time, discounting the news, stepping out to dance.

[1] Lars von Trier's 2011 movie *Melancholia* is about a wedding party held in the shadow of the end of the world.

should i message tris a photo of the sandwich i made yesterday? a sandwich inspired by a video he sent me last weekend while our friends were working out how we could simultaneously watch Cats (2019). what should i do with all this leftover parsley? i don't have insta but xan's linked her accounts so i see, twice, her post about having a few hours to do writing and moisturise. in a few days it will be ten years since the deepwater horizon exploded. what was it chris said about stereolab? murray knocks on my door to say sian's mum sent us each an easter package. he presses one ear a few times and says aw i guess yours doesn't work and we laugh and i close the door. in the mailbox is a note from the pharmacist: sorry but ritalin scripts expire after six months. i had a text saying the psych will call, don't come in, but she doesn't. often i dream about existing within a large crowd. three to five million barrels, depending on who you ask. on the weekend there'll be quizzes. the main thing i've learned is that crisps are good in sandwiches.

A SELFLESSLY EVACUATED SPIRIT

David Thomas Henry Wright

The following was computer-generated by a Javascript poetry generator inputted with the transcript of Queen Elizabeth II's Coronavirus Speech, addressed to the United Kingdom on April 5th, 2020. It was then human-edited.

Everyone faced disease duties:
　　none responded,
　　none resolve,
　　none characterise as essential.

Everyone reminds the globe:
　　commonwealth before nation,
　　wishes around pride,
　　science from sense.

Everyone lost feeling:
　　changes in expression,
　　the day-to-day self-discipline of the frontline,
　　hard businesses assuring advantages will be drawn after.

Everyone in the grief hour:
　　the slow years and parcels and opportunity and future,
　　the financial effort not remembered,
　　already a lost symbol.

Glasgow, Scotland GMT.

Olathe, Kansas GMT -5 hours.

Petaling Jaya, Selangor GMT +8 hours.

My husband and I are in Kuching, Sarawak at GMT +8 hours. His parents, siblings, sister-in-law are here; one sister and her family in Adelaide at GMT +9.5 hours. My parents, brother and wife are in Petaling Jaya, across the South China Sea. Katie, our elder daughter is in Glasgow; Emily, our younger daughter is in Olathe. They are students.

Kuching is a red zone with 178 known positive COVID-19 cases, 12 deaths. We have been under a nationwide Movement Control Order since 18th March and a state curfew from 7 p.m. to 7 a.m. since 24th March.

The Director-General of Health tells us the largest clusters of positive cases in Malaysia are those who participated in large gatherings: a *tabligh* in Kuala Lumpur, a church retreat in Kuching and a wedding in Bangi which infected people across five generations. He appeals to us not to stigmatize these groups for they are suffering terribly. Loved ones have died; relatives and friends in critical condition.

Groceries are delivered by an international student studying at a public university. He wears a mask, calls my husband 'Sir,' then rushes off. We spend hours washing and wiping the goods, finally leaving them on the verandah; apples, potatoes, ginger and canned food balancing on the rail; okra, brinjal, broccoli, carrots, cauliflower and eggs laid out like at an outdoor market. Then we shower.

Every morning, I wake up and check my phone. People have been busy in different time zones.

We had a video call the other day. It was Katie's birthday. Past midnight for us, Katie had just finished her lambing shift; Emily was in between dance classes with her professors in Iowa City via Zoom. We don't know when we will see each other in person again.

Yesterday was sunny, so I took a break from preparing online lectures and bathed our dogs. My husband, a wildlife biologist, took photographs of a crimson sunbird. We learned a Malayan tiger in the Bronx Zoo had contracted COVID-19.

Today, the British Prime Minister is in the ICU. The Malaysian Prime Minister will tell us in three days if the Movement Control Order will be extended. The American President tweets. We're staying home, working, living. But we're keeping track of developments in different time zones. This is all we can do.

AFTERWORD: IN HOMAGE TO INCOMPLETENESS

Julia Predergast

In writing, I feel I'm often thrown into unpredictable territory. I go to places that, frankly, I'd prefer not to be. I feel that this is necessarily the case if I'm writing anything that is, well, worth writing. A writing colleague and friend wrote to me, at the very beginning of the crisis, explaining that she was 'self-isolated, randomly enough, as the result of a fellowship in a writers' house'. She added: 'I'm writing lots of SEX, which is a little weird?' My response (in full) read: 'Not weird. Who chooses?' Later, I wrote again. I said I'd just sent a new story out. I explained that when I finished it, and read it a last time, I felt estranged from it, as if I was reading someone else's work.

Is this how we feel when we write into the unknown, only to come to know it and eventually unknow it? My traditional research addresses something close to this issue: meta-level experiences of creative writing processes. Two theories in particular guide my theoretical musings: the *unthought known* (from psychoanalysis) and *ideasthesia* or sensing concepts (from neuroscience).[1] Together, these theories assist me in articulating my understanding of a phenomenon I cannot prove except through experience: the experience of dreaming scenarios that are associatively connected to problems I am trying to solve in the creative work, the experience of remembering things that are seemingly (logically) unrelated to the evolving creative artefact, only to discover they are intrinsically, associatively tied to the themes and issues I am grappling with. I wonder: *Why on earth am I dreaming this? Why in the world am I thinking about that, now?* Each night, as I read the submissions, I felt that in some delightfully over-intimate and sustaining way, I was privy to aspects of the authors' unthought known or, at the very least, to the ways in which they had ideasthetically imagined their unthought known, in the current context.

On my last day in the office, before the university closed its doors, I was recording a lecture for first year fiction-writing students, bracing myself for the transition to online learning – 'transition', such a polite term, so unrepresentative of the truth of experience, as inept as 'transition' in childbirth. I'd bet that no woman who has given birth coined that term.

The lecture I was working on was a new one: Radical shortness – the challenge of brevity, focusing on 'sudden fiction', short-shorts, slice of life narrative. I opened the lecture with this quote from the God of Transitions – Lydia Davis (1983: 230):

> What is certain, in any case, is that we are more aware of the great precariousness and the possible brevity of our lives than we were in the past, our lives being actually more precarious than they used to be, and for this reason, perhaps, we express not only more despair but also more urgency in some of our literature now, this urgency also being expressed as brevity itself.

I included this quote as a way of connecting the learning material to our current climate, explaining to the students how the lecture would be structured for online delivery and my rationale for 'chunking' the lecture into chapters, focusing on authors and theorists of the form, followed by meta-analysis of the set readings and related exercises. At least, this is what I was trying to explain, in relation to the quote from Davis. Only I found myself becoming overly emotional, which is hardly unusual but not the point. I was recording per slide, at eight pm in a ghost university on the cusp of lockdown. I would choke, and re-record, and choke again. But *why* – re-record, that is? Who was I kidding that this wasn't overtly emotional subject matter for writers, for writing students? Davis' words were gutting because I felt she was speaking directly to me, through me, to the students, and she seemed, eerily, to be writing about our lives, *now*, and about the relationship between life and form, in a way that was some kind of acute 'flash forward' to what we are living. I was airborne: How could it have seemed so impossible that we might live this?

I am deeply interested in the relationship between what I see as the haunting incompleteness of human experience and short form writing. This, together with the unforeseen challenges of COVID-19, as well as the lure of coming together as writers, is the impetus for this book. In the lecture, I prompted students with a question from Gordon Weaver: 'in how small a space can [we] create the *felt presences* that animate successful stories [or poems]?' (1983: 228, my emphasis). *Felt presences* – I was reeling – the world becomes groundless in these words. I dwelt on this with the students, which really means, I recorded myself repeating it in the early evening grey of my Melbourne office. I said it over and again – *felt presences* – until I could feel one of the students from the future, listening from home, eye-rolling me: *Okay, okay we get it.*

'But do you?' I wanted to know. 'Do you, really, get it?' *Where are you?* I wanted to add. I was missing them already and they weren't really gone, yet, because this lecture had not actually happened, at least not for them. Already I was hyper-skeptical about this out-of-time world. In the old world I prefer face-to-face learning. I opt in for the real rather than the virtual, synchronous rather than a-synchronous – another polite term, a well-mannered or at least deferential way of saying that we are no longer permitted to exist or occur at the same time. Hence the profound importance of felt presences, in words. I'm inclined to remind the students, one more time, but I know it's too much.

This book focuses the brevity of form in 'sudden' writing, aimed at capturing our individual and collective experience as a composite picture. I am indebted to Robert Shapard and James Thomas (eds), for the term 'sudden' and to the contributions and ideas in their co-edited collection: *Sudden Fiction* (1986: xvi). As a preface to this collection, Shapard and Thomas include a very short story by Robert Coover, which begins: 'ONCE UPON A TIME, suddenly, while it still could, the story began' (1986: vii, emphasis in original). Shapard and Thomas acknowledge that the title of the collection arose from a suggestion from one of the contributors, Robert Kelly (1986: xvi). They also note the etymological origins of the term 'sudden': 'Without warning, from the Latin *subire*, to steal upon. Unforeseen, swift' (1986: xvi).

The term is entirely appropriate to the contributions in this book, which were collected in just nine days. *In The Art of Time in Fiction*, Joan Sibler (2009: 5) suggests that '[a]ll fiction has to contend with the experience of time passing'. When I talk to students about writing, I often talk about tiny telling details, concrete and specific details, being 'in scene'. It's pretend time, right? I talk, too, about the importance of managing shifting temporalities, anchoring the reader – ideas in pretend time. What's my point? The writing in this book seems to be somewhat obsessed with details and their place, in time. And with suddenness...

Each night, as I read the entries I meshed them in my mind, entries from near and far, words describing things that are 'foreign' and familiar to me. I think of how my own life has, in some respects, become tinged with foreign-ness. I think of the contributions that made me sob outright. I think of how I felt compelled to read them again, and again, trying to reconcile the emotional response with the content. In so doing, I remember a moment I've shared with many students, a *real* story about myself, as an undergraduate in a tutorial room on one of the upper floors of Monash Uni's Menzies building – reading a poem I didn't understand, sobbing outright and uncontrollably, excusing myself to collect myself. Later, I learned the poem was a lesbian love poem. Later, I reconciled my outburst with understanding – it was a day or so after Mothers' day, my beautiful Mum had died, recently, and I had a new baby girl. I didn't 'understand' the poem; except of course I did, because I understood love between women. 'Don't worry if you don't 'get it',' I tell the students. 'Ask yourself why the words make you feel the way they do? Get to the bottom of *that*...'

The relationship between words and meaning is entirely arbitrary and so, how, this magic? That is to say, what do our invisible ties to each other look like on the page, *now*, when the meaning of words is shiftier than ever? How do we see what we see; how do we know what we know, and don't know, or have not yet thought? My unthought known is undergirded by the contributions to this book, my imaginings, forever tinged. I think about how so many of the entries focus a kind of conflict – feelings, rights, responsibilities, duties – where to draw the line and where's the grey? I think of how this climate makes us other to ourselves – how it makes strangers, and foreign ideas, feel homely. I wonder if this makes me a cultural relativist, or whether I'm thinking more universally about these things. Am I a COVID-19 relativist? It is the willingness, in the contributions to the call, that overwhelms – the bold acts of exposure and solidarity in words that are no longer arbitrary.

I talk to undergraduate students online, synchronously, in 'Collaborate' sessions and via email – except they're not sending me email, they're sending me letters. In the 'Collaborate' session, I tell them I understand that they are desperate to write creatively and I hear them, so I've added a creative nonfiction option to the traditional essay questions. They want examples. How can I take the themes and issues in the weekly modules (Australian Writing and Cultural Change), and use them as a springboard for a work of creative nonfiction? I tell them about my beautiful Aunt and dear friend, warrior for mothers, champion of messy love and creativity. She died just prior to the enforcement of rules about large gatherings. 'We can't gather to celebrate and mourn, together,' I tell the students. 'If I were to write a work of creative nonfiction, about that, I might springboard from the module: Stories of war and conflict, but write about this, *now*.' The generosity of undergraduates, the tenderness of their ideas... I mourn that we can't gather in 'realtime'.

As I'm writing 'this' a dear colleague, who has become a dear friend, sends me a poem in four parts, written by a doctor. She writes: 'This might be the poem of the pandemic'. I include an extract from part two – 'Antiviral Cocktail: A Sequence' by Amit Majmudar (2020):

> 2. *An American Nurse Foresees Her Death*
>
> I stepped out of a kill-zone shaped like a bedroom
> then went home to sleep in my garage.
> This hand that sponged the fever off a body
> waves at my kids through the living room window.
> [...]

> Nurses I know are nursing nurses
> through the never-ending fevers
> ending them. That will be me soon,
> one or the other, or one then the other.
> At sign out last Friday, we didn't say
> bed numbers. We said first names.

As I read Majmudar I think of Fred Chappell's observation regarding the self-containment of the short form: 'The self-containment of the short-short is incomplete [. . .] it inhabits a larger world which it must take pains to imply. And the underscored knowledge that a larger world may obtrude upon it lends to the short-short both its inherent fragility and its peculiar toughness' (1983: 227, 227-228).

These twin concepts, fragility and toughness, are an apt preface for Majmudar's 'explanation' of the impetus for his poem:

> I myself am a practicing physician, but my main concern right now is my sister, an infectious disease physician who currently runs Cook County's HIV clinics in the South Side of Chicago. [. . .] These related poems, though not specifically pertaining to her, have emerged from the welter of emotions surrounding this catastrophe. (Majmudar 2020)

Each of us, managing our own contingencies, tempering our imaginings, or not, fashioning something from them. . .

My eldest daughter is a critical care nurse. She is looking after those in the stronghold of the virus, their lungs 'underwater'. This is her training. For nurses, surely, it's a vocation. When I think of her, there, I see all of her but mostly I see her hands and I hear her voice. Overnight, and in the early hours, she sends me a number of text messages. She is not a poet. She is a straight-shooting, kind-strong nurse:

> My COVID patient nearly died twice, last night.
> I'm so sweaty. I'm totally wrecked.
> She was on max ventilation.

The ventilator is on a closed circuit.
I had to break the ventilator circuit twice.
So we could better oxygenate her blood.
I had to clamp her breathing tube to connect her
to the medication so I didn't spread Corona.
This virus doesn't discriminate.

These messages are followed by some unrelated, hysterical, asides. This is the regular rhythm of our interchange. It ends in a sword-fight of inappropriateness because that's our friendship. I bring it back in the end, tell her I've cooked her some meals for driveway collection. *Disinfect hands. Place meals in the boot. Wave. No touching. NO touching. Distance. Disinfect hands.* I tell her if she gets sick, I'll come and nurse her – my youngest child protests. I see her in my mind's eye, after she pulls out of the driveway, and I smell her scent – it feels like a memory of those I love who are gone. I don't want to think that thought but there it is, nevertheless.

When she gets home, she calls. I hide in my bedroom for our 'virtual' dinner party. I think about how she swoops in and sorts things out, if I *can't*. I remember one day in particular, leaving for work, dishing out a million everyday instructions. She sipped her tea in her nursing scrubs: *Mum. Go to work. I've got this. We're not here to fuck spiders.* I guess I should mention my other children, or delete this paragraph, in case they read this when I die, and object that I'm playing favourites. Already, they weigh and measure, dealing backhanders about my attention to the nurse. It's in jest but still. . .. They say: *I know she's in the frontline, but. . .*

I should put them out of their misery and tell them love is not even or fair. On this subject, my grandmother (mother to nine children, and a paediatrician), was asked in an interview if she loved all of her children equally, or something along those lines. She said: *No. I love most, the one who needs to be loved most, at any given time.* Or something along those lines. As I re-read this, today, the direction of *most-love* has shifted. 'I can't deal. . .', one of my other children sobs. She's been working long hours in the supermarket, so she has contact, but no realtime connectivity.

I began writing something 'sudden' from the nursing-daughter's text chain, from our subsequent talking and my unthought known imaginings – twisting formlessness through fiction, trying to make something... *palatable*. It's not there yet and I'm not sure this one will get there. The sentences are jamming too hard. I mean jamming but, as I read this, I think I'm unintentionally implying enjambment because I can't get her original out of mind. I have geometric patterns on a floor rug, longing and its (sometimes hysterical) applications – I have hand-sanitiser and gin, strangers dying intimately. Something about a holding pattern. At the moment it's awful and I'm not sure I can make it good. I'm trying though because I'm a writer – we are writers – what else can we do?

I leave you with a question from H E Francis, focusing 'tone and situation' which, he argues, is 'where story and poem meet' (231, 232). Francis asks: 'Can our time achieve the one-to-one density of parts (each with multiple meanings) in a density of the whole (with multiple interpretations) of earlier parable and allegory' (232). To my mind, this book bears witness to that question and, perhaps, to the shattering of the self and its composite subjectivities.

A few days before submissions close, a dear writer-friend emails but not to discuss writing. She says: 'I'm totally fucking over this social iso thing. I think of all the wines and all the bars I've experienced with you and the longing is palpable. Palpable!' I write back to her, a rebound email, a one-minute ode about palpability and longing, in concrete memories, *I want*... dancing on train platforms, serenading, nudity. If anyone is stalking my email it will sound as though we are having a love affair. What's my point? *Realtime. Flesh.*

It's the second last day before submissions close. A precious writing-friend, US based, born and raised in the Philippines, emails to say she can't submit because she can't write, and she talks about why, her current 'thinking positions'. I cut some extracts from her email and send them back to her as a Word document. I say: I think you *are* writing. There is some back and forth, as these things go, her wondering if it's good enough, me in wonder at how I'm transported by her words. I've never been to the US, nor do I know anything about the Philippines, but in her words, I have been and I do know. In a final email, she writes:

> When I sent in the latest revision, I felt like there was something 'kulang', as we say in Filipino, regarding the last line. I just tried googling an English translation of the word about what I mean and of all the definitions, I think the closest I mean to say is that the last line was wanting.

Today, submissions close. I write three new works of sudden fiction. I write madly. I don't want this to end. I don't like endings. It's a *thing*. When I break from writing I make a pot of tea and read the new submissions. At one of them, I cry wildly. It is perhaps one of the most everyday ones. I cry because I'm there, in the unfettered everyday of that world. For a moment, I'm not here. It's me, over there, seeing your incompleteness, feeling it as my own.

A dear writing-friend messages in the hangover, after the call for contributions has closed. She says she missed the deadline. She also explains that she wasn't sure about submitting because: what if her words hurt the person referred to in her writing? She says she couldn't bear it. She sends it to me but not for the book. I rebound:

1. I love you
2. This is a superb piece of writing – the vortex-like rhythm.

She comes back: 'If you'll take it, I'll submit it here. I'm drowning in my lack of agency right now. I feel like a prisoner in the things I can't say for fear of making everything worse. That's no way to live'.

Thank you to all contributors, for heeding the call to lay bare your 'thinking positions', for breaking me and sustaining me at a time when, perhaps, we all need to be reminded of what it is to be broken and how, as the ground shifts at every turn, we might sustain ourselves.

One of my children is a muso. He started biomed but chose music, instead. He is the one who finds me the most annoying. He tells me, deadpan: *Why do you have to be so 'on' all the time? It's so annoying...* Just now he was singing a new song. 'What *is* that?' I said. He played it for me on his phone, telling me about the band from the Folkie, who wrote it. I said: 'Are you going to learn it' (guitar)? He said: 'I just did, but I need someone for the other bits. Violin. Or I could just loop it...'.

In this book I hear us, looping, offering 'the other bits' – writers questioning the composite picture of themselves, fractured and indivisible, in an altered world. I read the entries and think, again, about interconnectedness and the willingness to share. I hear writers, in *kulang*. I know that whatever I say, here, or in the stories I write across this time, it will feel *wanting*, because it is, *I am...*

But then, all of our voices together, making something that is *not-wanting*. There is no antonym for not-wanting that will capture that – Sufficient? Acceptable? *Pfff.* I'm not suggesting that because it's not-wanting, it's complete. I don't believe it is and perhaps it shouldn't be, but *please* – the felt presences...

Write boldly. Go gently. In solidarity.

Julia.

[1] I focus on neuroscientist Professor Danko Nikolić's concept of *ideasthesia*, coupled with the concept of the *unthought known*, originating with Christopher Bollas, Professor in Literature and a psychoanalyst. Ideasthesia is drawn from Nikolić's definition, which arises from the 'Ancient Greek words idea (for concept) and aesthesis (for sensation). Hence [...] the term ideasthesia [or] *sensing concepts*' (Nikolić 2016, emphasis in original). Ideasthesia provides a means for understanding the way writers sense ideas in metaphorical and associative ways. Nikolić (2016: 4, 5) is concerned with 'what is happening in the minds of people while they experience art': arguing for 'a particular relationship between the depth of meaning and the intensity of sensation'. I'm interested in the concept of ideasthesia as it applies to producing art – in order to bring narrative to life

LIST OF WORKS CITED

Bollas C 2017 *The Shadow of the Object: Psychoanalysis of the Unthought Known*, Routledge, Abingdon

Chappell F 1983 'Fred Chappell', in R Shapard & J Thomas (eds), *Sudden Fiction: American Short-Short Stories*, Gibbs Smith, Layton UT: 227-8

Davis L 1983 'Lydia Davis', in R Shapard & J Thomas (eds), *Sudden Fiction: American Short-Short Stories*, Gibbs Smith, Layton UT: 230

Francis HE 1983 'H. E. Francis', in R Shapard & J Thomas (eds), *Sudden Fiction: American Short-Short Stories*, Gibbs Smith, Layton UT: 231-2

Majmudar A 2020 'Antiviral Cocktail: A Sequence', Rattle (April 9): https://www.rattle.com/?s=majmudar&submit=Search Nikolić D 2016, "Ideasthesia and Art." www.danko-nikolic.com/wp-content/uploads/2016/02/Ideasthesia-and-art.pdf.

Nikolić D 2016, 'Ideasthesia and Art' [To appear in: K Gsöllpointner et al (eds) 2016 Digital Synesthesia. A Model for the Aesthetics of Digital Art, De Gruyter, Berlin/Boston]. Available at: www.danko-nikolic.com/wp-content/uploads/2016/02/Ideasthesia-and-art.pdf

Silber J 2009 *The Art of Time in Fiction*, Graywolf Press, Minneapolis MN

Weaver G 1983 'Gordon Weaver', in R Shapard & J Thomas (eds), *Sudden Fiction: American Short- Short Stories*, Gibbs Smith, Layton UT: 228-9

in an experiential way, in order, that is, to show rather than tell, I argue that writers sense concepts, plotting ideas *as* sensory data. This "thinking position" draws me to Bollas' concept of the unthought known. I come up with the term ideasthetic imagining, suggesting that this process is an act of forgetting (I the author) and remembering (the I of experience). Bollas argues that 'aspects of the unthought known – the primary repressed unconscious – will emerge during a psychoanalysis, as a mood, the aesthetic of a dream, or in our relation to the self as other' (2017: preface). In a similar way, ideasthetic imagining leads to the emergence of aspects of the unthought known that are consonant with a mood, a dream aesthetic, an *othered* sense of self.

Julia Prendergast writes long and short form fiction. Her novel The Earth Does Not Get Fat was published in 2018 (UWA Publishing: Australia) and her short stories feature in the current edition of Australian Short Stories (Pascoe Publishing). Julia's research has appeared in various publications including: New Writing (UK), TEXT (AU), Testimony Witness Authority: The Politics and Poetics of Experience (UK). Julia is a Senior lecturer in Writing and Literature at Swinburne University, Melbourne, and the current Chair of the Australasian Association of Writing Programs (AAWP). She is an enthusiastic supporter of interdisciplinary, open and collaborative research practices.

Alberta Natasia Adji is currently a creative writing PhD candidate at Edith Cowan University. She has published two novels, *Youth Adagio* (2013) and *Dante: The Faery and the Wizard* (2014), some short stories in *Jawa Pos*, and refereed articles in *Prose Studies*, *Life Writing*, and others. She holds a bachelor's degree in English literature and a Master's Degree in Cultural Studies from Universitas Airlangga, Surabaya, Indonesia.

Patrick Allington is a writer and editor. His novel *Rise & Shine* will be published by Scribe Publications in June 2020. His novel *Figurehead* (Black Inc. 2009) was longlisted for the Miles Franklin Literary Award, and his short fiction, essays and criticism have appeared widely. He has taught politics, Australian culture, communications, creative writing, and publishing and editing, most recently at Flinders University. He is a former Commissioning Editor for the University of Adelaide Press.

Kay Are is a writer and researcher with interests in multimodal poetry and fiction; experimental writing processes and translation; experiential pedagogy; and posthumanist, feminist and materialist approaches to all the above. Collaborations and discussion welcome: kay.are@unimelb.edu.au

Fin Ash is a screenwriter, Australian Writers' Guild member and PhD candidate (RMIT). She has a Master of Screenwriting (VCA), has had screenplays in development and did a work placement at a long running television drama. Her plays have been produced in Britain and Australia and won awards. Her creative practice research PhD project interrogates atypical fidelities in adaptation seeking to give equal weight to Jane Austen's proto-feminism, sociopolitical interests and experimental narrative techniques as well as the plots and characters. Her general research focus includes cultural policy, non-exclusionary representational diversity in mainstream film and television, and social justice through popular culture.

Cassandra Atherton is an award-winning scholar and prose poet. She was a Harvard Visiting Scholar in English and a Visiting Fellow in Comparative Culture at Sophia University, Japan. Her most recent books of prose poetry are *Pre-Raphaelite* (2018) and *Leftovers* (2020). She co-wrote a scholarly book on prose poetry for Princeton University Press and co-edited the *Anthology of Australian Prose Poetry* (forthcoming). She is currently working on a book of prose poetry on the atomic bomb supported by an Australia Council Grant.

Pooja Mittal Biswas is the author of five books of fiction and poetry. They have been reviewed and interviewed in *The Age*, *The Australian* and ABC Radio National's *The Book Show*, and have been anthologised in both *The Best Australian Poems* and *The Best Australian Poetry*. They have written for *Writer's Digest* and have been widely published in literary journals such as *Meanjin*, *Hecate* and *Jacket*. They were selected as the national representative for UNESCO's Babele Poetica project. Currently, they are pursuing a PhD in English from the University of Sydney.

Donna Lee Brien is Professor of Creative Industries at Central Queensland University, where she is Academic Leader of the Creative Arts Research Training Academy.

Gayelene Carbis is an award-winning writer of poetry, prose and plays. Her first book of poetry, *Anecdotal Evidence* (Five Islands

Press) was awarded Finalist – International Book Awards 2019. Recent Shortlistings/prizes: poetry – MPU; My Brother Jack Poetry/ Short Story; Montreal; ACU; short story: *ABR, The Age, Meniscus Best Small Fictions*; and various poetry/prose awards. Gayelene teaches Creative Writing; English/EAL; and is Poet-in-Residence in schools.

Ash Cassel is an Honours student at Southern Cross University. Her thesis examines the role of visual articulation and flux in writing her trauma memoir. She found that drawing helped her come to terms with her in/completeness of human experience and with the in/completeness of her story. Her memoir tells the unravelling and revealing experience of revisiting a site of trauma. Drawn from her Honours, this is a memoir piece that explores the evolving and interwoven nature of trauma and closeness.

Janice Caulfield is a PhD student in the Creative Writing program at Curtin University. Her work has been published in *CINDER* and she is the author of the non-fiction book *A Victorian Woman's Journey to New Zealand* (2014), Ngaio Press.

Rebekah Clarkson is the author of *Barking Dogs* (Affirm Press, 2017). Her short stories have appeared in publications including *Griffith Review, Best Australian Stories* and *Something Special, Something Rare: Outstanding Short Stories by Australian Women* (Black Inc.). She coordinates the Writing Centre at the University of Adelaide and teaches fiction writing in Australia and overseas.

Katharine Coles has published seven collections of poems, most recently *Wayward* (Red Hen Press, 2019). Her memoir, *Look Both Ways*, was released in 2018 by Turtle Point Press, which will also publish *The Stranger I Become: Essays in Reckless Poetics* in fall 2020. In the US, she has received awards from the National Endowment for the Arts, the National Endowment for the Humanities, and the Guggenheim Foundation. She is a Distinguished Professor at the University of Utah.

Emilie Collyer lives in Melbourne's west, on Wurundjeri land, where she writes poetry, plays and prose. Her writing has appeared most recently in *Australian Poetry Journal, Witness Performance* and *Cordite.* Award-winning plays include *Contest, Dream Home* and *The Good Girl.* Emilie also works as a dramaturg and text consultant. In 2020 she is starting a PhD in creative writing at RMIT.

Shady Cosgrove is the author of *What the Ground Can't Hold* (Picador, 2013) and *She Played Elvis* (Allen and Unwin, 2009). Her short works have appeared in *Best Australian Stories, Overland, Antipodes, Southerly,* and Spineless Wonders anthologies. She teaches creative writing at the University of Wollongong, Australia.

Dave Drayton is an amateur banjo player, founding member of the Atterton Academy, Kanganoulipian, and author of *E, UIO, A: a feghoot* (Container), *A pet per ably-faced kid* (Stale Objects dePress), *P(oe)Ms* (Rabbit), *Haiturograms* (Stale Objects dePress) and *Poetic Pentagons* (Spacecraft Press). He lectures in Creative Writing at UTS.

Oliver Driscoll's debut poetry collection, *I don't know how that happened* (Recent Work Press), was published in 2020. He won the 2015 Melbourne Lord Mayor's Creative Writing Award for Narrative Non-fiction and was shortlisted for the 2019 Dorothy Hewett Award for an Unpublished Manuscript. His work has been published in *Kill Your Darlings, Sleepers, Meanjin, Cordite, Rabbit,* and *Red Room,* among other places. Oliver co-runs the *Slow Canoe Live Journal.*

Dr **Willo Drummond** is a poet and sessional lecturer in creative writing. She writes about creativity, human and non-human animals, gender, and the fragile landscapes of identity. Her work is published in Australian and international journals including *Cordite, Mascara, Writing from Below, Meniscus, Bukker Tillibul* and the US little magazine, *Yellowfield.* In 2020 she sheltered in place in Darug and Gundungurra country in the NSW Blue Mountains.

Katrina Finlayson is a creative writer and researcher, working mostly in creative nonfiction. Katrina's personal and critical essays have been published in *Meanjin*, *TEXT*, and *Axon*. Her writing explores ideas about strangeness, place and displacement, home and travel, and the nature and significance of memory and identity.

Christie Fogarty is a PhD Candidate at Griffith University, Queensland. Her current project is a work of fiction exploring the boundaries of the self, and rape mythology.

Annette Freeman is a writer living in Sydney, Australia. Her work has appeared in a number of Australian and international journals, and she was a 2018 Pushcart Nominee. She has a Master of Creative Writing from the University of Sydney and is presently working towards a Doctorate of Arts at the same university.

Laura Fulton is a writer, teacher and researcher based in Melbourne. Born in the Mississippi delta region of Arkansas, this fourth-year PhD candidate is currently exploring how the adopted person may address issues of identity, origin and belonging through creative writing experimentation. She is also working on a fiction novel addressing themes of disruption, longing and loss among an imagined family history, how we cope with those experiences and ways of looking forward and back.

Sarah Giles is a postgraduate student at Swinburne University of Technology where she is studying creative writing. Her short stories and personal essays have been published in the *Victorian Writer*, *Lip Magazine*, *Underground Writers*, and *Melbourne Noir Cards*.

Stephanie Green is a widely published Australian writer and lecturer at Griffith University. Her work has appeared in *TEXT*, *Griffith Review*, *Axon*, *Westerly*, *Island*, *Overland*, a variety of anthologies, and leading international scholarly journals. She has also received literary awards, including *The Age* Short Story Award (1991) and the Hal Porter Short Story Award (2012). Her books include a volume of collected prose poems, *Breathing in Stormy Seasons* (Recent Work, 2019) and a selected short fiction, *Too Much Too Soon* (Pandanus, 2006). Her research includes studies in gender and transmedia fantasy narrative and she is a member of the international research network, Imagining the Impossible: https://www.imaginingtheimpossible.com/

Dominique Hecq grew up in the French-speaking part of Belgium. She now lives in Melbourne. Dominique writes across genres – and sometimes across tongues. Her creative works include a novel, three collections of stories, and nine volumes of poetry. Among other honours such as the Melbourne Fringe Festival Award for Outstanding Performance, the Woorilla Fiction Prize, the Martha Richardson Poetry Medal, the New England Poetry Prize, and the inaugural AALITRA Prize for Literary Translation (Spanish to English), Dominique is a recipient of the 2018 International Best Poets Prize.

Eileen Herbert-Goodall has had many pieces of non-fiction and short fiction published in various magazines, journals, and international anthologies. She is the author of a novella titled *The Sherbrooke Brothers* (Moonshine Cove Press, 2017). Her second novella is due out in late 2020. Eileen teaches writing at the University of the Sunshine Coast, Australia, and holds a Doctorate of Creative Arts.

Suzanne Hermanoczki is a writer and teacher of creative writing. Her writing has been published in local and international publications including *Australian Multilingual Writing Project, Cha: An Asian Literary Journal, TEXT* and the anthology *Verge*. She has a PhD in Creative Writing from the University of Melbourne, where she currently works.

Paul Hetherington is Professor of Writing in the Faculty of Arts and Design at the University of Canberra, head of the International Poetry Studies Institute (IPSI) and one of the founding editors of the international online journal *Axon: Creative Explorations*. He founded the International Prose Poetry Group in 2014. He has published and/or edited 27 books, including 13 full-length poetry collections and nine chapbooks. Among these are *Moonlight on Oleander: Prose Poems* (UWAP, 2018) and *Palace of Memory* (RWP, 2019). He won the 2014 Western Australian Premier's Book Awards (poetry) and undertook an Australia Council for the Arts Literature

Board Residency at the BR Whiting Studio in Rome in 2015-16. He was shortlisted for the Kenneth Slessor Prize in the 2017 New South Wales Premier's Awards.

Christine Howe is a writer and academic who teaches at the University of Wollongong. Her first novel, *Song in the Dark,* was published by Penguin and her short works (poetry, lyric essays, microfictions) have appeared in the *Griffith Review, Cordite* and various Spineless Wonders anthologies.

Sreedhevi Iyer is the author of *The Tiniest House of Time* and *Jungle Without Water.* Her work has been shortlisted for the Penang Monthly Book Award in 2017 and also been nominated for a Pushcart Prize in the US. Her work has appeared across the world, including the US (*Hotel Amerika, Drunken Boat, Ginosko Literary Journal, Asian American Literary Review,* The *Bellingham Review, The Writer's Chronicle*), the UK (*Free Word Centre*), Hong Kong (*Asia Literary Review, Cha: An Asian Literary Journal*), Malaysia (*Everything About Us*), Sweden (*Two Thirds North*) and more.

Stefan Jatschka is a PhD candidate at Griffith University. His research investigates travel writing and mother-son relationships. He has been published in *TEXT, Talent Implied* and *Getamungstit.*

Luke Johnson is a Lecturer of Creative Writing at the University of Wollongong.

A journalist for more than forty years working in Australia and the UK, **Sue Joseph** (PhD) began working as an academic, teaching print journalism at the University of Technology Sydney in 1997. As Senior Lecturer, she now teaches in creative writing, particularly creative non-fiction writing. Her fourth book, *Behind the Text: Candid conversations with Australian creative nonfiction writers,* was released in 2016. She is currently Joint Editor of *Ethical Space: The International Journal of Communication Ethics.*

Helena Kadmos is the Academic Coordinator for Internships with the McCusker Centre for Citizenship at the University of Western

Australia. Her fiction and non-fiction appears in *Westerly*, *Meanjin*, *Eureka Street* and *Meniscus*. Helena's research on representations of women in the short story cycle can be found in various journals including *Short Fiction in Theory and Practice*, *Outskirts* and *JASAL*.

Nat Kassel is a PhD student at Griffith University and a freelance journalist. Her research areas are the gig economy and the precarity of work.

Katrina Kell is an Australian writer and researcher. She is the published author of two young adult novels, *Juice* and *Mama's Trippin'*, and her short fiction, essays and articles have appeared in anthologies, journals, conference proceedings and magazines. She has a PhD in English and Comparative Literature (Creative Writing), and in March 2020, she was awarded an Australian Society of Authors' mentorship supported by the Copyright Agency Cultural Fund for her historical novel manuscript 'Anatomy of an Artist's Model.' She currently teaches in the Career Learning Spine at Murdoch University.

Michelle Kelly is a Sydney-based scholar and emerging creative and critical writer, with recent publications in the *Sydney Review of Books* and *Writer's Bloc*.

Nigel Krauth has published four adult novels (two of them national award winners) and three teenage novels, along with stories, essays, articles and reviews. He is head of the writing program at Griffith University, Queensland. His research investigates creative writing processes and the teaching of creative writing. He is the General Editor of *TEXT: Journal of Writing and Writing Courses*: www.textjournal.com.au

Jeri Kroll is Emeritus Professor of English and Creative Writing at Flinders University, South Australia, Adjunct Professor of Creative Arts at Central Queensland University and an award-winning writer for adults and young people. Recent books are *Workshopping the Heart: New and Selected Poems* and a verse novel, *Vanishing Point*, shortlisted for the Queensland Literary Awards. *Research Methods* *in Creative Writing* and *'Old and New, Tried and Untried': Creativity and Research in the 21st Century University* are recent critical books. Forthcoming from Red Globe Press (Palgrave Macmillan) is *Creative Writing: Drafting, Revising and Editing*, co-edited with Graeme Harper. She is a Doctor of Creative Arts candidate at the University of Wollongong.

Matt Lewin is a musician, music therapist and emerging writer. His first submitted piece 'Please Shut the Door Quietly' was published in *Meanjin* and explored the transformational experiences he has experienced and observed while working in palliative care. Matt also produces music under the moniker Spacecadet Lullabies.

Joshua Lobb is Senior Lecturer in Creative Writing at the University of Wollongong. His stories have appeared in *The Bridport Prize Anthology, Best Australian Stories, Animal Studies Journal, Griffith Review, TEXT* and *Southerly*. His novel, *Remission*, won the LitLink Unpublished Manuscript Award in 2014, as well as two residential fellowships at Varuna, the Writers' House. His 'novel in stories' about grief and climate change, *The Flight of Birds* (Sydney University Press, 2019) was shortlisted for the 2019 Readings Prize for New Australian Fiction. He is also part of the multi-authored project, *100 Atmospheres: Studies in Scale and Wonder* (Open Humanities Press, 2019).

Rose Lucas is a Melbourne poet and academic in graduate research at Victoria University. Her first book, *Even in the Dark* (UWAP 2013), won the Mary Gilmore Award; her second book *Unexpected Clearing* was also published by UWAP in 2016.

Gay Lynch works as an adjunct academic at Flinders University, Adelaide, publishing essays, hybrid memoir pieces, novels, papers and short stories. *Unsettled*, her Australian frontier novel, was launched by Hannah Kent in late 2019. You can find her recent shorter works in *Best Australian Stories, Bluestem Journal, Edições Humus Limitada, Glimmer Press, Island, Meanjin, Meniscus, Griffith Review, Westerly, TEXT* and *Sleepers Almanac*. From 2011-2015, she was Fiction and Life Writing Editor at *Transnational Literature* e-journal.

Elizabeth MacFarlane is a Senior Lecturer in Creative Writing at the University of Melbourne where she teaches Theory for Writing, Graphic Narratives and Short Fiction. Elizabeth is Co-Director of Twelve Panels Press, and recently departed Co-Director of the Comic Art Workshop. Her book *Reading Coetzee* was published in 2013 and her co-edited collection *Superhero Bodies* was published in 2019.

Sophie MacNeill is a writer and PhD candidate at Griffith University, where she is working on a fiction-memoir hybrid manuscript. Her short fiction has appeared in *Talent Implied: New Writing from Griffith*, *Bareknuckle Poet Annual Anthology*, and *ACE Anthology* (Recent Work Press).

Alan McMonagle has written for radio and published two collections of short stories. *Ithaca*, his first novel, was published by Picador in 2017 as part of a two-book deal. His second novel, *Laura Cassidy's Walk of Fame*, was published in March of this year. He lives in Galway, Ireland.

Alyson Miller teaches literature, writing and culture at Deakin University, Melbourne.

Carol Mills is an emerging writer with a primary interest in creative nonfiction. Carol is a postdoctoral adjunct fellow at Curtin University. She is currently seeking a publisher for her creative work 'The Pilot's Wife' and is the author of the blog *52 Pages*. The blog explores connections between theory, writing and visual art.

Sudesh Mishra is the author of *The Lives of Coat Hangers* (Otago UP, 2016). He now lives, works and writes in the city of his birth, Suva.

Judi Morison writes short fiction, poetry and creative nonfiction, and is working on a second novel while waiting for a publisher to snap up her first. Her short fiction can be found in the *2019 UTS Anthology* and in the upcoming *2020 UTS Anthology* and *2020 ACE*

Anthology. She is Editorial Assistant for *Dreaming Inside: Voices from Junee Correctional Centre*, an annual anthology of writing by Aboriginal inmates.

Molly Murn holds a Master's in Creative Arts, an Honours degree in Dance, and is currently a PhD candidate in Creative Writing at Flinders University. Her debut novel *Heart of the Grass Tree* was published with Penguin Random House (Vintage) in 2019. Molly's poetry is published in various anthologies, including *Transnational Literature* and *Overland*. She lives in the Adelaide Hills.

Peta Murray is a writer-performer and teacher, best known for her play, *Wallflowering*. Recent works include *Missa Pro Venerabilibus: A Mass for The Ageing*, *vigil/wake* and *On Our Beach*. A Vice-Chancellor's Postdoctoral Research Fellow in the School of Media and Communication at RMIT University, Peta's focus is the application of transdisciplinary arts-based practices as modes of inquiry and forms of cultural activism. Critical writing includes contributions to *Axon*, *Fourth Genre*, *New Writing*, *RUUKKU* and *TEXT*.

Pablo Muslera teaches creative writing, communication and foundation studies courses at the University of South Australia, where he's also an Honours supervisor. He's current Co-Editor of the Reviews section of *TEXT*.

Peter Nash is studying for a PhD in Creative Writing at Griffith University. He is a regular contributor to *TEXT*.

Janet Newman lives in Horowhenua, New Zealand. This year she completed a PhD in creative writing at Massey University with a thesis titled 'Imagining Ecologies: Traditions of Ecopoetry in Aotearoa New Zealand'. Her poetry has been published widely in journals and anthologised in *Manifesto Aotearoa: 101 Political Poems* (2017). Her poetry collection *Unseasoned Campaigner* was a runner up in the 2019 Kathleen Grattan Award.

Charli Newton is a dual UK-Australian writer living in Perth. She has a BA in English Literature from Exeter, a Masters in Creative

Writing from Oxford, and is a PhD candidate in Creative Writing at UWA. She was 2019 Writer in Residence at the Fremantle Arts Centre, and is signed to literary agency AM Heath.

Dr **Sarah Pearce** is an independent researcher, editor, poet and performer from Adelaide. Her work appears in *Aeternum, Outskirts, Meniscus, Writing from Below* and *TEXT*. She has held residencies at Adelaide City Library and FELTspace gallery and performed at Blenheim Festival and Adelaide Fringe Festival. Her writing concerns the female body and embodiment, relationships, the Gothic, writing back and queer narrative(s).

Dr **Mary Pomfret** works and lives in Bendigo, Australia. Mary is an honorary researcher at La Trobe University and her short fiction and poetry have been published widely. Her debut novel, *The Hard Seed*, was published in 2018.

Antonia Pont writes poetry in Melbourne, on Wurundjeri land. She has published work in many anthologies and journals, and is also an essayist, scholar and practitioner. Her recent book *You Will Not Know in Advance What You'll Feel* appeared with *Rabbit* in 2019.

Rachel Robertson is Senior Lecturer and Deputy Head of the School of Media, Creative Arts and Social Inquiry at Curtin University, Western Australia. She is the author of *Reading One Thousand* (Black Inc) and co-editor of *Purple Prose* (Fremantle Press), *Dangerous Ideas about Mothers* (UWAP) and *Manifestos for the Future of Critical Disability Studies* (Routledge).

Deedle Rodriguez-Tomlinson was born and raised in the Philippines. Her poems, reflecting her peripatetic life, appear in *Under the Storm: An Anthology of Contemporary Philippine Poetry* and in the special literary issue of *Silliman University Journal*, as well as Tomas, the literary journal of University of Santo Tomas in the Philippines. Her essays and recipes have been published in the book *Potluck: Hidalgo Bonding*. She is program manager for New York Writers Workshop and lives in Brooklyn with her husband Tim.

Shannon Sandford is a PhD candidate of Life Narrative in the College of Humanities, Arts, and Social Sciences at Flinders University, South Australia. Shannon's thesis explores hybrid webcomics as a new autobiographical form connecting graphic narrative with digital and social media. Shannon is also a member of the Flinders Life Narrative Research Group.

Jane Scerri is currently in her third year of a DCA in creative writing at the University of Western Sydney. She has published several short stories and academic papers and is currently working on her second novel. Her main interests are feminism and representations of female desire in contemporary Australian literature.

Pushcart Prize-winning poet **Ravi Shankar** is author, editor and translator of 15 books, including *W.W. Norton's Language for a New Century* and *The Many Uses of Mint: New and Selected Poems 1998–2018* (Recent Work Press). He currently holds an international research fellowship from the University of Sydney and his memoir *Correctional* is forthcoming with University of Wisconsin Press in 2021.

Barrie Sherwood is a fiction writer and an Assistant Professor of English at Nanyang Technological University, Singapore.

EJ Shu is an Australian-Canadian poet whose recent work appears in *Cordite Poetry Review, Plumwood Mountain, Antiphon, Poets Reading the News* and elsewhere. She is currently pursuing a PhD in the School of Media and Communication at RMIT University.

Hazel Smith is an Emeritus Professor at Western Sydney University. She has published four volumes of poetry including *Word Migrants*, Giramondo, 2016, and numerous performance and multimedia works. She has written several academic books including *The Contemporary Literature-Music Relationship: intermedia, voice, technology, cross-cultural exchange*, Routledge, 2016. In 2018, with Will Luers and Roger Dean, she was awarded first place in the Electronic Literature Organisation's Robert Coover prize for the work *novelling*. Her web page is at www.australysis.com.

Mary Paige Snell has published stories in various literary magazines, including *No Tokens, Best of Ducts, Nerve Cowboy,* and *Specter.* She has performed with John Moran and Ridge Theater, in venues such as Lincoln Center, and can be heard on the Point Music (Philip Glass) Recording of Moran's Opera 'The Manson Family' with Iggy Pop. She is currently working as an actor on various productions with Whole Picture Films. She studied at Tisch School of the Arts/ ETW and The Visual Arts Department of NYU, and writing at New York Writers Workshop with Tim Tomlinson. She is from Norwich VT/ Hanover, NH and lives in New York City.

Shane Strange's writing has appeared in various print and online journals in Australia and internationally. He is the author of two chapbooks, *Notes to the Reader* and *Dark Corner.* His first collection of poetry *All Suspicions Have Been Confirmed* will be released in late 2020. He is publisher at Recent Work Press and has been Festival Director of the University of Canberra's Poetry on the Move poetry festival since 2018.

Stayci Taylor is a lecturer at RMIT University, where she pursues her creative practice research with the non/fictionLab in the school of Media and Communication. Her critical and creative interests are screenwriting, script development, creative writing and, more recently, non-fiction, especially through the lens of diarology.

Tim Tomlinson is co-founder of New York Writers Workshop and co-author of its popular text, *The Portable MFA in Creative Writing.* He is also the author of *Yolanda: An Oral History in Verse, Requiem for the Tree Fort I Set on Fire* (poetry), and *This Is Not Happening to You* (short fiction). He teaches in the Global Liberal Studies Program, NYU.

Dr **Sonya Voumard** is a non-fiction writer and journalist with three published book-length works. They include a novel and two works of creative non-fiction: *The Media and the Massacre* (2016, Transit Lounge) was long listed for a 2017 Stella Award and a 2018 Nita B Kibble Literary Award. *Skin in the Game, The Pleasure and Pain of*

Telling True Stories was published by Transit Lounge in March 2018. This is an excerpt from her new memoir-in-progress titled *Tremor.*

Amelia Walker has published four poetry collections, most recently *Dreamday*. From 2017–2019, she served as secretary on the AAWP executive board. She is presently employed on a teaching-only contract at a South Australian university.

Jen Webb is Distinguished Professor of Creative Practice at the University of Canberra, and Co-Editor of *Axon: Creative Explorations* and the literary journal *Meniscus*. Her most recent poetry collection is *Moving Targets* (Recent Work Press, 2018), and *Flight Mode* (co-written with Shé Hawke) will be launched in October this year.

Connor Weightman has been published in *Westerly, Cordite* and *Plumwood Mountain*. He's currently working on a PhD about the poetic representation of the problem of oil.

David Thomas Henry Wright won the 2018 Queensland Literary Awards' QUT Digital Literature Prize and 2019 Robert Coover Award for a work of Electronic Literature (2nd prize). He has been shortlisted for multiple national and international literary prizes, and published in various academic and creative journals. He has a PhD (English and Comparative Literature) from Murdoch University and a Master's (Creative Writing) from The University of Edinburgh, and taught Creative Writing at China's top university, Tsinghua. He is currently Co-Editor of *The Digital Review* and Associate Professor (Comparative Literature) at Nagoya University.

Christina Yin lives in Sarawak, Malaysian Borneo with her husband and two mixed-breed dogs. A senior lecturer at Swinburne University of Technology, Sarawak Campus, she is also undertaking her doctoral studies at the University of Nottingham Malaysia. Her fiction and nonfiction writing have appeared in *Anak Sastra* and *eTropic Journal*, among others.

ACKNOWLEDGEMENTS

I would like to acknowledge the contribution of all authors, including those who do not appear in this book. We received hundreds of entries across a nine-day submission window. There were many works of significant literary merit that we were unable to include. This book is dedicated to all authors – thank you for your profoundly moving writing.

My heartfelt thanks to the co-editors of *The Incompleteness Book*: the entirely excellent Shane Strange, editor and publisher at Recent Work Press, and to Queen of Ace, Distinguished Professor Jen Webb, Centre for Creative and Cultural Research, University of Canberra. Thank you, dear comrades, for editing this book with fortitude and signature *elan*, in record time. I am inordinately grateful for your acuity (and for the hilarity).

Thank you to the Australasian Association of Writing Programs (AAWP), the peak academic body representing the discipline of Creative Writing in Australasia, for pledging financial support for this project. We are collectively indebted to Dr Eileen Herbert-Goodall, Dr Daniel Juckes, and Dr Helena Kadmos, who provided invaluable administrative and editorial assistance in support of this project – thank you Eileen, Daniel and Helena, for being meticulous, reliable and relentlessly pleasant, and for your respectful and astute handling of author contributions. We are grateful to the editorial team at *TEXT Journal*, for embracing an earlier version of this initiative – thanks in particular to Professor Nigel Krauth, Griffith University, General Editor at *TEXT*, for indomitable creative vision and signature good energy.

www.ingramcontent.com/pod-product-compliance
Lightning Source LLC
Chambersburg PA
CBHW020322010526
44107CB00054B/1945
9780648834380